Supernatural in Cornwall

Michael Williams

BOSSINEY BOOKS

To the memory of Pip, whose words were an omen, and Tex, a faithful friend, who shared more than one strange experience.

CONTENTS

			Page
Introduction			1
1.	TONACOMBE	An Old Lady	5
2.	CLEAVE CAMP	Strange Sounds	11
3.	PENFOUND MANOR POUNDSTOCK CHURCH	Kate Murdered Priest	15
4.	BOSCASTLE	Witchcraft	24
5.	ST. NECTAN'S GLEN	Hermitage & Waterfall	30
6.	BOSSINEY	Midsummer Eve Lights	34
7.	TINTAGEL	Charmer	40
8.	ST. AUSTELL	Spiritual Healer	44
9.	ROSEANNON	Curing a Dog	53
10.	SALTASH	UFOs & Healing	58
11.	LOSTWITHIEL	The Squire	65
12.	NEAR PROBUS	AA Box Mystery	68
13.	BODMIN MOOR	Ghost Car	73
14.	POLZEATH	Strange Events	79
15.	ST. ISSEY	Violent Forces	85
16.	LITTLE PETHERICK	Ghostly Meetings	91
17.	WITHIEL	Clairvoyant	94
18.	FALMOUTH	Doomed Sailor	100
19.	NEAR CROWLAS	Premonition	104
20.	ST. JUST	Hoof-beats	108
21.	ST. BURYAN	Unexplained Noises	111
Postscript			117

First published in 1974
by Bossiney Books
St Teath, Bodmin, Cornwall

Second Impression 1975
Third Impression 1977
Fourth Impression 1978
Fifth Impression 1979

ISBN 0 906456 16 9

Printed in Great Britain by Penwell Ltd. Parkwood, Callington, Cornwall

ILLUSTRATIONS

PLATES 1, 2, 3, 4, 5, 6, 7, 8, 10, 11, 12, 19, 20, 23 & 24 by BRYAN RUSSELL

9, 13, 14, 15, 17, 18 & 21 by RICHARD HAWKEN

16 by MALCOLM S. HENCHLEY

22 by ROBERT ROSKROW

Cover by Topsie Lee

INTRODUCTION

Tracing the genesis of this quest for the supernatural is difficult. The truth is our memories retain little. A man may live through twenty-five thousand days and nights, but the odds are he will recall less than two hundred. Many of our waking hours are like leaves trodden underfoot and forgotten.

I suppose the nearest thing to a springboard for me was a strange experience at Bossiney by Tintagel. Legend has it that King Arthur's round table lies beneath Bossiney Mound and that it comes to the surface one night a year in shimmering silver. Midnight on Midsummer Eve, they say, so I went along Midsummer Eve 1965, three other people went too, plus a tan and white terrier, Tex by name. We never saw King Arthur's table - common sense told us it probably never existed - But we had the surprise of our lives. If I had been alone, I should have said " Mere imagination!" As it was, the others, from a different vantage point, shared the eerie spectacle. In retrospect, most significant of all, was the behaviour of the dog Tex - a pugnacious little character, yet that night, for a few moments, courage deserted him.

From somewhere around a quarter past midnight, I never laughed again about the supernatural; never again adopted a cynical Doubting Thomas attitude. But more of this later.

Perhaps, though, the roots are deeper back . . .

It was wartime; Hitler's bombers were pounding London, so my uncle was in Cornwall, as a break from the blitz. He was a lean man. (Later when I saw Alastair Sim on the cinema screen I remembered him). Now I know, he was a great uncle ; I realise too, he was probably the first person who made me think about the possibility of another, unseen world. He, not the parsons and the Sunday School teachers, made me think seriously about something beyond the grave.

We were living at 5 Barwis Hill, Penzance; one of a sloping terrace, a house with black and cream painted doors and windows. Below the Recreation Ground, where as boys we played cricket and football, and above the Roman Catholic church whose bell,

I always thought, had a sad sound. Uncle - I never gave him his full title - was sleeping in my bedroom at the back of the house. That week I emigrated to a camp bed downstairs.

"Danger's going to come near," he said one morning at breakfast, "but you'll be safe."

"What do you mean?" we asked.

"I saw a monk in black, and in mourning, last night. He stood at the foot of Michael's bed and told me so."

Uncle left at the week-end. The following week Penzance had one of its few air-raids; a bomb landed on Barwis Hill demolishing two houses at the end of the row. We were lucky; only shattered glass and a shock. Those bombed sites remained for a long time, skeletons reminding me of the monk in black. When I switched off the bedroom light I wondered if he would reappear. In time I almost forgot him, yet never completely. Whenever the subject of spirits was raised, I thought of him. He became a kind of secret, a special piece of information reserved for close friends.

I am a Cornishman and proud of my nationality. There is a Celtic something in the bones of this land, in some of its people, too. Material and mystical are cunningly mixed and the line dividing past and present often grows blurred. Charles Simpson, a fine painter and no mean descriptive writer, said of the Cornish landscape: "Tracing the history of these relics is like reading a book whose pages grow blurred and confused as the plot unfolds. An empty cottage or farm-steading tells of the failure of some small human endevour: a family has died out, a building becomes uninhabitable through disuse or lack of repair. The giant warren of a mine where pit-shafts gape beneath crumbling masonry, where the drone of engines is heard no more and kestrels hover round their lofty housing, marks the conclusion of a larger enterprise - no more is earth shaken by the tramp of oxen turning the windlass of the cage in earlier days . . . The noise of labour has died away in silence. The pages of the book read slowly as the writing fades. A doomed hut, roofless, buried in a tangle of briar, would escape notice were it not for the chippings of flint arrow-heads lying round it on soil turned by the plough. The writing is almost blotted out. Legend and myth are vague as a twilight sky dreaming over stone circles on the hills; never will time unravel their mystery; gone is their message, like the oracles of the wind blown to heaven with the leaves through which they spoke. A solitary menhir rears its grey length towards the sky and points - at shadows."

Dramatic language, but then Cornwall - or parts of it - is a dramatic place. If you judge by the sandy beaches and the picturesque coves, you are only getting part of the picture. Housing estates may be devouring our land, the grasp of tourism may be growing greedier but in the more remote regions a haunted and haunting atmosphere remains: the real spirit of Cornwall clings to the 20th century.

Economics, too, played their part in fashioning my search. From the outset, I resolved to meet people, to visit places. The wider the net, the greater the expense. Literally, I drew a line across the Tamar.

"Are you attempting to prove the existence of ghosts?" somebody asked.

I have attempted to prove nothing.

Instead the journalist inside me has endeavoured to report events accurately and clearly, content to let the events and the people concerned, speak for themselves. After that Midsummer Eve, I cannot be anything but a sympathetic listener. Moreover, I distrust that word 'objective.' Also I admit, that I find it hard to believe that sixty or more people, who have come forward, are either downright liars or mentally disturbed.

"As far as I am concerned one is always living on the edge of two worlds, particularly in Cornwall, where divisions seem to be thinner and basic forces stronger." Thus wrote the sculptor and author Sven Berlin in a letter to me. "De la Mare said he did not feel safe again until he had crossed the Tamar - going east. You have chosen a rich mine to re-open. I have every sympathy with your work and wish you success in your explorations. I don't for a minute think you are a crackpot, but I do think you will attract a great many crackpots around you; it will be a devil of a job sorting out the pots that are not cracked, who are really quite serious."

Sven Berlin was correct. The mail, coming through the letter-box, did contain some weird epistles. One correspondent claimed second sight to the extent of 'seeing' winners of races as the horses paraded in the ring before going down to the starting stalls - presumably he is now a millionaire. Another foresaw a rail disaster but lacked the courage of her convictions to send a warning telegram. There were accounts that looked all right on paper but which shrunk in a face-to-face interview. There were others, which on investigation revealed inaccuracy, and possibly invention. There were instances where enquiries came to a cul-de-sac. In one parish I ran into a collective brickwall: a string of denials. In another, a person seeking the sale of a house,declined to discuss the possibility of hauntings. A few people laughed it off. Only two - one a parson - did not have the courtesy to reply. On the whole I met a ready spirit of co-operation. Few attempted embroidery. If they had wanted to invent, they would have created more colourful, more gruesome episodes. Nobody mentioned clanging chains or bodies rising from their graves.

Typical was the reaction of a woman from Bude.

"Would you describe yourself as having both feet on the ground?" I enquired.

"I've spent a good deal of my life mucking out stables" she retorted, "you can't be more down to earth than that!"

"What kind of people have they been?" a friend asked.

Looking back, I can find no common denominator, save blue eyes. Understandably there have been more women than men. "Men might be afraid of people thinking them soft," as one woman put it. Men, who did admit to supernatural experience, however were anything but soft. A farm worker, a regular soldier, a retired Naval Commander, a planter from Malaya, an RAF policeman, a former High Sheriff of Cornwall and two Canons of the Church of England - these were only some who had no hesitation.

One evening early in January 1974 a clairvoyant visited us in our little cottage behind the hotel at Bossiney. A sensitive character, a potter and a painter, she loved delving into the magical and the mystical things of life. Her partner had died a year ago, but she assured us she had seen him quite recently.

After a little hesitation I allowed her to tell my future, hesitatingly because though I am sure some people have the gift of foreseeing, I cannot somehow believe that cards can be linked to Fate and the unknown.

"Michael," she said, looking up from the carefully placed cards on the coffee table, "you're going to write a book about the supernatural and it's related to Cornwall."

I had no reason to suppose that she knew about my supernatural notes lying in that bottom drawer.

Within a fortnight I was looking at a small wooden box in Tintagel Church containing her ashes. She had died in her sleep on the date of her late partner's birthday. "It's not a sad occasion," said Sonia my wife, as we walked from the shining, wet churchyard. "Pip was always half in this world and half in the next."

Before dinner that evening I went to the bottom drawer and looked at the hillock of notes, and by the end of the month I started writing, attempting to turn them into a book . . .

TONACOMBE 1

An Old Lady

It was a cold October morning and I was having a lunchtime drink and snack in the bar of The Bush Inn at Morwenstow.

" If you're looking for supernatural stories " said the landlord, " you should talk to David Waddon-Martyn. He's had some strange experiences. His family home is Tonacombe . . . only half a mile away . . . but he's not there now. He lives somewhere down in Cornwall."

I wrote to David Waddon-Martyn that evening: c/o Tonacombe - " Please Forward." Ironically, ' somewhere down in Cornwall ' turned out to be only a few minutes away from our hotel at Bossiney.

A week later I was heading northward to Tonacombe with David Waddon-Martyn driving his Wolseley. A biting east wind, whipping white horses across a choppy sea, sent a shiver over the countryside. Gulls hovered in a field and we were conscious of autumn suddenly tightening its grip. The approach to Tonacombe is quaintly called Street. Hidden from the road, is one of the finest examples of a 15th century manor in the whole Westcountry. S.P.B. Mais thought it " worth crossing a continent to see." One literary theory is that Charles Kingsley used Tonacombe as the setting for the chapel in *Westward Ho*! Dating from the reign of the first Elizabeth, it has three courtyards and a walled garden. Inside, the hall is open to the roof. There is a minstrel's gallery and a priest's hiding place.

Born in Ceylon in 1930 and educated at Downside, the famous Roman Catholic public school, David Waddon-Martyn was a keen sportsman: cricket, rugger, hockey and tennis. A good slice of his adult life has been spent abroad, initially National Service with the 1st Battalion of the Oxfordshire and Buckinghamshire Light Infantry; then four years were spent in Rhodesia, three in the Police Force and one in tobacco. After Rhodesia he spent four years planting in Malaya. Back in England, he worked with Peter Scott for two years at Slimbridge, and since then he has been living in Cornwall with his wife and children. He is the twin son of the late Captain William Waddon-Martyn, J.P., a former tea planter and owner of Tonacombe.

"My first occasion of being contacted by something was about eleven o'clock one night, when I was walking through the panelled parlour, its window faces the Pleasance, a walled garden. I was suddenly confronted with a distinct *knock . . . knock . . . knock*, upon the outside of the window. I looked towards the window but there was no sign of any being in the vicinity and nothing else could have made this solid kind of noise . . . just like a human knocking on glass. I went outside, thinking possibly someone wanted to attract my attention, but I found no-one in the garden. Also, the gate leading to the Pleasance was locked with a chain and padlock. I passed this incident off . . . nevertheless I felt that *something* had caused it, but more than that, I could not say. With a shrug, I went to bed.

"A few nights later I was walking through the Pleasance after having visited some friends in the parish. The time was again about eleven p.m. - and I was suddenly confronted with a distinct knocking, similar to the previous occasion, upon the window of my bedroom, only this time, the knocking came from within the house. I looked up towards the window and called 'Hello, is that you, Mother?' The room was unlit but I thought my mother could have been up there, passing through to her room. There was no reply, so I proceeded through the back door leading from the Pleasance, along a passageway to see where my mother was. She was sitting in the white Jacobean room watching television. I asked her whether she had been upstairs within the last half hour ; 'No' she replied. This made me believe that someone or something was trying to attract my attention. I hadn't mentioned these two knocking episodes to anyone. Not because I didn't think people would believe me but because I thought it might frighten others in the house. So I let it be.

We were now talking in a bedroom at Tonacombe once occupied by David Waddon-Martyn. There was a goblin-like knocker on the door ; and two religious statuettes above the bed. Thirteen pictures punctuated the oak pannelled walls. My eyes moved from a fox's brush to a stuffed curlew. "This is the Kempthorne coat of arms" said David Waddon-Martyn pointing to a spot high on the pannelling. The view from the mullioned window encompassed the Pleasance. A bent ash stood by the lawn ; a starling hovered over a grey stone bird-bath and nearby was an ancient Celtic cross. It might have been a picture from *Country Life* but my attention was drawn back to the bedroom.

"The position of the bed's changed. It was over here." David Waddon-Martyn strode across the wooden, rugless floor, indicating the original position. "Otherwise the bedroom's more or less as it was . . . It was about three o'clock in the morning, shortly after the second series of knocking . . . It was from this bedroom that I'd heard them. I sat up in bed. I know I was fully awake. There was no case of it being a dream. You can put that possibility aside." He had guessed my unspoken question. "Then I heard a noise like material being moved, like a parson wearing his cassock. Dark as the room was, I could see a figure of misty appearance, such as a figure seen through net curtains. The figure seemed as if it were under some illumination; of course it wasn't but that's how it seemed to me at the time. It was standing at the edge of my bed . . . the distinct image of an old lady in Stuart period costume. There were movements of the lips and there was expression in the eyes. It was definitely trying to tell me something; the lips were moving a lot, but the rest of the body was still. I managed to say 'Who is that? What do you want?' and then I must admit, I was frightened. Although this being was saying something, there was no sound of a voice from it.

"I lay down in bed and pulled the blankets over my head; on doing this, I felt the sensation of the blankets being pulled down the bed. In actual fact, they had not moved but the presence was of them being moved from the bottom of the bed. Straight-away I put on the light and slept with it on for the rest of the night.

"I rather wish I hadn't put on the light, since I now believe she was definitely wanting my help or wanting something, or wanting to tell me something. I slept in a different room after this, as quite honestly I was a bit frightened . . . although now I feel that she was perfectly harmless, and that she probably sought me as a medium or contact for some purpose which I may now never know. Maybe though, I'll sleep in this bedroom again and hope that she'll reveal what she was trying to say."

David Waddon-Martyn thinks his three a.m. visitor may have been Katherine Kempthorne, who was buried in Morwenstow Church on February 14, 1613.

"I believe she died a couple of days before that on the 12th, and in this very room. The experience had occurred during that very bad winter of 1963, in the month of February, I can't be sure of the exact date but can only suggest she appeared on the anniversary of her death." Katherine married John Kempthorne of Tonacombe at Chudleigh in 1558. Her husband died in 1591 and she married again three years later. Her second husband was Degorie Tremaine and, until his death in 1600, they lived over the border at Tavistock. Widowed for a second time, Katherine returned to Tonacombe and spent her last thirteen years there.

An hour later, David Whaddon-Martyn and I were in the parish church. Katherine Kempthorne's bones rest in the Kempthorne tomb. There are several other ancestral links here; not least the reredos, a segment of the 1904 restoration containing three attractive engravings by John Baptist Jackson, gifts of Lawrence Martyn then of Tonacombe. They are over the altar, and above them is another gift, an original drawing by the 17th century artist Giovanni Baptista Piazzetta.

David Whaddon-Martyn settled himself in the family pew.

"Has anybody else seen Katherine either here or back at Tonacombe?"

"My mother who sleeps next to the bedroom I occupied, where Katherine died, only this month heard knocking on her door. Rather like the knocking I'd heard, an inexplicable knocking, too solid for anything but a human knock. Mother told me that one night in 1952 she felt the presence of what could have been the same person, standing at the end of her bed staring at her, and then leaving the room. Going by what she told me its characteristics were similar to my own experience; although there was no noise of material such as a gown being moved, she had this same feeling of being studied. Nothing really unusual happened, but Mother suddenly felt the absence of it as it left her room to go into mine. I wasn't in residence at the time; I was in Egypt.

"There've been other instances. All the family children were brought up at Tonacombe. An aunt of mine, a sister of my father's experienced the occurrence of a little man entering her bedroom from the farm side. He was dressed in a black coat, waistcoat and his breeches did up with many buttons to the knee. I believe she said he was bald. He was observed by her standing right over her head. I can't say any more as my aunt's now departed too."

"My sister's eldest son, when he was about four years old, slept in the room next to the bedrooms my mother and I had." He woke up suddenly one night and asked his mother: 'What is that little man doing in my room?' That must have been about 1961.

"There was also a housekeeper, who for many years used to look after Tonacombe: a Mrs. Vanstone. She related how she once saw an Elizabethan dressed woman with a big bunch of keys standing near the fire-place in the Great Hall.

" I believe all these things . . . the people concerned, in my opinion, were honest and sincere.

" In connection with my own particular meetings, when I am at Tonacombe I feel as if I am followed by someone from off this earth, but I always feel happy to be there and feel the place is most friendly, and, on leaving, I feel somewhat depressed. As for this feeling of being followed, I noticed that our cat at Tonacombe, on one occasion, saw me in the parlour, the room where I first heard the knocking on the windows, and its eyes got as big as saucers, a sign of extreme fright, before it ran away. I never found it for the rest of the day. This actually happened on several occasions and the cat each time, always seemed to be looking in my vicinity.

" Something happened outside the house too. There's a wood, about two fields away, where I took our old springer spaniel one day. We were on our way home, when suddenly she stopped dead on the path behind me, and, with fear in her eyes and her hair standing up, she barked and barked. It was a frightened bark, if you've heard one you'll know what I mean. This barking persisted though I was only say, twenty-five yards in front of her on the same path. She was staring at me or past me, but she would not move an inch ; neither would she come when called or enticed. This made me somewhat cautious, as she'd never reacted this way before and I could see nothing unusual. I walked back to her, and then continued up the path and called but again she refused to move and just carried on barking. I went along the path alone till I entered a field and, unknown to the dog, came up behind and called her. She immediately came to me and was delighted, but never again did she want to go through that wood. To this day, I believe it was something to do with the supernatural.

" Some people may say about these occurrences : 'Oh, it's your imagination playing games with you.' I disagree. Never once prior to any of these occurrences had I been thinking of ghosts. There was nothing further from my mind. I was very keen on shooting and fishing, and my mind was almost all the time on these pursuits.

" Since having gone through these experiences and, in particular, the happening in the bedroom, I do believe in the supernatural and would welcome further experiences. I would not cut the whole thing short next time.

" Ghosts, such as the average person knows them, are things that go bump in the night and are covered by sheets - some may be, but my own opinion is, that they're people who have not fulfilled an earthly life and wish to fulfil themselves by contacting someone whom they think is ideal and sympathetic. This may be because they love a place or are good people, or even because they have lost something and wish to find it before they can rest peacefully . . . There are certain wishes and commitments that can linger after death.

" Possibly, I am being directed by this old lady, to find something for her, which - if I do - would no doubt put her mind at rest. Maybe not. Maybe she just loves Tonacombe and prefers to go around as she had done long ago, and just wants me to know she is there.

" Either way, I'm grateful for these experiences. They've really awakened my interest in the past. I almost feel born out of my time . . ."

CLEAVE CAMP 2

Strange Sounds

There were dozens of sheep, some grazing, others sprawled out resting in brittle sunlight.

Ruins of an old farm house. Rubble and weeds; rows of silent, empty shabby buildings, here and there a broken pane of glass. Once they were billets or storehouses, latrines or offices. This is, or was Cleave Camp, high on the cliffs of North Cornwall, seven miles north from Bude.

My next destination might have been lifted from the set of a Hitchcock film. Prior to the outbreak of war and during it, Cleave accommodated both the Army and RAF.

"It had a grass airfield with the Army camp on the Bude side and the RAF camp on the Morwenstow side" one ex-serviceman recalled. "We used to fly single-engined aircraft, towing targets for the anti-aircraft gunners. Apart from the permanent staff, the Army personnel changed about every six weeks and there was anything from five hundred to a thousand in each new battery that came in. The RAF camp, including officers and maintenance workers, averaged about two hundred and fifty. WAAF personnel didn't arrive until late '42 or early '43, when they took over some of the wireless and domestic duties. Really it was quite a small airfield, only suitable for single-engined aircraft, although I recall, on one occasion, an American fortress landing in desperation, stopping only a yard from a hedge, with its petrol tanks empty."

When the war ended, the Territorials came here for their annual firing practice. After that, the camp was closed. Local traders, especially the publicans, complained bitterly.

"The Terriers often brought their wives and families to Bude for their holidays. While husbands became soldiers again for a fortnight, their families enjoyed themselves on the beaches." Three years later the camp reopened. But by now the planes were getting too fast for the Royal Artillery. Closure came again in the spring of 1960 and this time there was no reprieve.

One man, who knew Cleave during its war-time life, was Victor B. Smith, an RAF Police Corporal who, as a civilian, had spent ten years with Plymouth Corporation as a market inspector. Invalided out of RAF blue in 1945, he ran for five years his own business in conjunction with a sub-post office. Now, he was living in semi-retirement.

"Can't keep out of business!" was his comment at Western Tors Cottage. This 300 year-old building, stands just above the River Yealm in South Devon. Several caves stand alongside the cottage.

"I was on duty in the Guardroom at Cleave. It was eleven o'clock at night and I found that one WAAF was still out, although all the girls were supposed to have booked in by that hour. I can still remember the girl's name, Ivy Flannagan. At about ten minutes past the hour, she arrived and I chastised her for being late. 'I can't help it,' she said, 'I can't sleep when I get down to the billet." I asked her why and she replied that she thought the Polish airmen were coming onto the WAAF site at night and were banging on the Nissen hut, and the girls were frightened."

Further conversation with an ex-Cleave Camp WAAF showed this was no exaggeration. I interviewed Constance Luckes * in the lounge of *The River Yealm Hotel* at Newton Ferrers. A parrot eyed us from his perch, while a cat curled before the fire. Outside heavy rain rattled the windows, and in the harbour below boats bobbed about. Newton Ferrers is a picturesque village on the South Devon coast, a favourite haunt for sailing and sea fishing. Constance Luckes, a Devonian, bespectacled and extremely neat, gave the impression of a reliable witness In a conversation devoid of extravagant gesture and dramatic tone, her words came slowly, carefully, yet confidently; gradually too, a firm belief in the power of the supernatural emerged.

"I was a motor transport driver at Cleave" she recalled, "and rumours began to build up very quickly. Apparently there were noises in one of the WAAF huts. Things came to a head, when one of the girls fainted and had to report sick. She told the MO about the noises but he laughed it off and told her to pull herself together. Then another WAAF reported sick - a kind of nervous condition for the same reason - and she reported the matter to her WAAF Commanding Officer. But like the MO the WAAF Commanding Officer dismissed the story as a

* Victor Smith and Constance Luckes, though contemporaries at Cleave, and now living only a few miles from each other, did *not* meet again until *after* our interviews.

piece of nonsense. The girls, however, continued to be troubled by the noise, and some who lived locally refused to stay in the hut and went home at night!"*

The RAF Commanding Officer, aware of spreading apprehension, detailed Victor Smith to keep watch on the hut.

"The first night at approximately 11.15 p.m. I lay in the long grass beside the Nissen hut equipped with a powerful torch and my revolver in case of trouble." For our interview, Victor Smith was wearing a sports jacket and corduroy trousers and as we talked in his cottage at Yealmpton, I was attempting mentally to reconstruct the Cleave setting all those years ago. A fortnight earlier, I had visited Cleave Camp. The huts had been on the seaward side of the camp, overlooking Stanbury Cove. Only their concrete bases remained; the buildings had been sold at a public auction a few years back.

"Not a sound anywhere" Victor Smith continued, "when suddenly above my head was a banging on the iron sheets enough to wake the dead. The girls all started screaming, but as it took me by surprise, I lay still, and did nothing. Within a few minutes it happened again . . . this time I was ready. I had got my revolver out and my finger was on the button of the torch. My torch was on before the noise had stopped. I flashed the light around; a rabbit scurried away . . . there wasn't a soul anywhere. I went around to the door of the hut, and made myself known to the girls who let me in. I made a thorough examination of the hut but could find nothing that I thought would make sufficient noise. I even tried banging the leather heel of a girl's shoe, but could make nothing like the noise.

"I duly reported this to the CO next morning, who was most definite that it must be stopped."

But there was no stopping the mysterious nightly bombardment of this one WAAF hut. Incredibly neither of the other huts suffered and mystery deepened in that a particular girl, a pretty blonde, somehow managed to sleep through the din. Though, according to Constance Luckes, the girl was "in a bath of perspiration, in a state of great agitation, and really gave the impression of being in a trance, or under some control." In an effort to solve the mystery, the girl was removed to another hut and the bombardment followed her; whereas her normal abode,

*"Though I wasn't in the hut which had the disturbances, like the rest of the girls, I was terrified," is the memory of another WAAF, now Mrs. E. Turner, of Eastham, Cheshire. "When the noises first started, it didn't seem too bad; excuses were made for them, mice or somebody playing a practical joke. The girls became so tense that I can remember two or three of them fainting in the NAAFI on the same day."

in her absence, experienced no alarms. On returning to the first hut, however, the girl was pursued by uproar while the second hut went back to its original peace.

There was no escape on night duty either. " One night she was in the operations room, and her colleague was scared stiff by the terrible noises that rained down on the building.

" The whole investigation lasted several weeks." Victor Smith reflected, " I spent almost every night on the spot. I found that if I had a night off and went to bed early, I would be disturbed to escort any girls who had a late pass because they were afraid to go there on their own. The girls' nerves were in such a state that it became necessary for me to escort five or six at a time to the toilets, while the knocking was in progress. The CO used to pull my leg, saying I was the only man who had such a job in the whole of the RAF !

" On one occasion I took one of my colleagues and he wouldn't stay. I vividly remember his remarks " - ' No, we're in Cornwall and although I've never believed it before, I've heard tales of being pixie led and I'm not taking any chances now.' " And no persuasion on my part would make him stay !"

" The situation became so acute, that one night the whole of the Officers' Mess assembled in the WAAF hut to witness the crisis for themselves. The pattern persisted ; concern spread throughout the camp, news of ' ghosts ' leaked out. Victor Smith, in a Bude cafe one evening, was asked, " How's the ghost hunting going ?"

Solution eventually came through a spiritualist ; a Corporal Green, who was in charge of the Parachute Section. It was necessary to keep the parachute materials at a consistent temperature. As a result, Corporal Green became a recluse-like figure often spending the entire twenty-four hours inside the walls of his section. He asserted that - through psychic forces - he was able to determine the cause and the nature of the noises. The mother of the blonde girl had died, (records quickly confirmed this fact) and the dead parent was endeavouring to warn her WAAF daughter of the dangers of an unsatisfactory relationship she had struck up with a certain man. The girl herself denied any knowledge of Spiritualism and, in the words of Constance Luckes : " was made thoroughly unhappy by the whole episode. She thought it unfair to be blamed for something about which she knew nothing and over which she had no control."

The Commanding Officer decided on a compassionate posting. The girl left Cleave. Peace returned to the WAAF quarters and a knock was never heard again.

PENFOUND MANOR 3

Kate

POUNDSTOCK CHURCH

Murdered Priest

From Bude, my supernatural trail switched south, away from the cliffs and the sea, down the twisting A39 into the countryside.

Five cows meandered on to the wrong side as I came to crossroads. "Penfound Manor 1, Week St. Mary 2," indicated a signpost pointing left. I turned the driving wheel accordingly, and it was about three-quarters of a mile up the road that I met a man walking. Carrying a raincoat, he was wearing a deerstalker hat and a frown.

Bringing the car to a halt, I unwound the window.

"Can you tell me the way to Penfound Manor please?" — I had once heard it described as 'the best hidden manor in the kingdom.'

The face, beneath the battered deerstalker, hardened into a deeper frown.

"Next right . . . then left . . . but you won't find it open."

"I have an appointment."

The man grunted and walked on.

"Thank you for your help."

But there was no reply.

"There is an idyllic old English home that belonged to an ancient family of the same name, the Penfounds of Penfound in the parish of Poundstock . . . in a dip in the land, at the source of a little stream, snuggling into the fold of the down, bedded into foliage, open to the sun, hummed about by bees, twinkled over by butterflies, lies this lovely old house."

That was how Sabine Baring-Gould described Penfound in 1898, the year of Kitchener and Omdurman.

As I came to the wrought iron tracery gate and looked across the flagstones, past the fountain, to the facade of Penfound itself, I almost felt as I did so, a sensation of travelling back in time. Autumn was already tinting the leaves and the face of the landscape. The afternoon sun sloped westward like a faint fire still smouldering. Diamond-glass windows glinted as my eyes travelled across the uneven roof of the house.

There are no Penfounds at Penfound today. As Stuart supporters, they had had their manor confiscated by the Crown in 1759. The last of the direct line, Henry Penfound, died in the local poorhouse in 1847. The inscription above the granite archway at Penfound reads : "In the yeare 1642." The e's, carved backwards, are a craftsman's clue indicating Royalist allegiance.

Since setting out on this supernatural journey across Cornwall, some things have changed : addresses in some cases have altered; properties have changed hands. A few people, like Pip, have departed this earthly life. But the essential facts remain : the evidence of people experiencing events outside the ordinary operation of cause and effect. This stays as strong as ever. Indeed, since interviewing and making my original notes, I have sifted the evidence carefully. Where people have been shy about their names appearing in print, I have omitted such information. Where there has been doubt, versions have not progressed beyond the notebook stage. From the first page to the last I have worked towards facts. This, therefore, is no work of fiction.

As far as Penfound is concerned, there have been changes since that afternoon when I stood looking at the glint of those diamond-glass windows. The manor then, belonged to Kenneth and Doris Tucker, who opened the house to the public during the holiday season. Then as many as 20,000 visitors passed through its doors. Today it is a private house once more, the property of Colonel and Mrs. Haynes.

"I don't believe in the supernatural," said Kenneth Tucker sitting in his dressing gown in front of a crackling, spluttering log fire in the Great Hall. He looked a very sick man and died only a few weeks after our meeting. "But I suppose you could say the supernatural in theory had something to do with our coming to Penfound. It was in the spring of 1957; I'd been unwell, and we were spending a holiday in Palma. There, we became friendly with a middle-aged woman, also on holiday. She was a palmist, a fortune-teller. Just for fun, I allowed her to read my palm, and she told me my whole life would change in the near future. She related I should have to give up my job and my home. Of course, I told myself, she couldn't possibly be right. After thirty-eight years in the bank and now a manager a man couldn't have been more set in his ways. But I was proved wrong. Later that year I suffered another bad bout of bronchitis, and the doctors told me to give up banking. They suggested Cornwall . . . and here we are!"

This, the Great Hall, until early Norman days, was Penfound's total structure, the fireplace and the chimney were added probably during the reign of King John, when, according to Kenneth Tucker, chimneys were first employed. Inside the chimney is a tiny shelf, containing a bottle, the contents of which are said to be holy water brought all the way from the Holy Land. It is also said if anyone removes the bottle the chimney will instantly collapse. "We haven't put it to the test," my hosts confessed. "The water may well come from the River Jordan . . . there is a River Jordan down at Boscastle." The window in the Great Hall is Elizabethan in both design and construction, some of its scarlet and blue glass in the border coming from Westminster Abbey.

As Doris Tucker took me from room to room, showing me various furnishings, explaining something of their background, I realised why this has been called 'the most beautifully furnished house in Britain.' And, as outside earlier, I was aware of an aura of the past, serenity which words cannot begin to describe. Tempo slackens, one feels a slightly different person, more relaxed, more leisurely. Yet there is no sense of being in a museum. "I should hate to live in one!" said Kenneth Tucker. "This is a home."

"This is not a stately home," the Tuckers wrote in their admirable guide, "built and fortified by some royal tyrant to ensure more rest for his uneasy head, or flung to some fawning lordling in exchange for dubious and probably immoral services rendered. Penfound was built slowly, gradually, by ordinary gentry for ordinary gentry to live in, and bring up their families in, and die. This house has witnessed dark deeds, petty quarrels, family feuds and great joys. Is there a prefab which has not? But here the merciful hand of antiquity has blurred the outlines and softened the harsh and angry voice, and may we acquire for a while the imperturable detachment of ancient things."

From the start of these investigations, I resolved to ignore legends, preferring to concentrate on present-day supernatural claims that could be checked and challenged personally. Once or twice a legend has tempted me to deviate from that resolution — not so much the legend, but claims coming in the wake of the legend as if they were giving flesh, blood and bones to the original. The story of Kate Penfound proved such an enticement. Kate fell in love with John Trebarfoote of Trebarfoote Manor, some three miles away, but the Civil War cast its shadow over such a match, for the Trebarfootes had supported Cromwell, and the Penfounds the King. The two lovers decided their only hope was an elopement and schemed accordingly. On the 26th night of April - nobody knows the exact year - Kate slipped from her bedroom via the solar window to John Trebarfoote, who was waiting in the courtyard. But the girl's father suddenly appeared — at which point legend offers alternative endings. One version is that Kate's father shot the young lovers as they stood locked in an embrace in the porch. Another is that the two men drew swords; Kate, in an attempt to separate them, was killed and both men died in the duel.

The Tuckers never saw Kate's ghost, but they were intrigued by the reactions of some visitors. Standing alongside the four-poster in Kate's bedroom, Doris Tucker told me of an incident during their first summer. "I was showing a party of people around the house and was explaining the legend in this bedroom, when I noticed a man and woman exchanging glances." 'My wife's psychic' the man explained later, 'and when we arrived at the gate just now, she didn't want to cross the courtyard.' 'I can't go in there,' she said. 'I know something dreadful has happened here.' On another occasion, two women visited Penfound, only to find they had come on the wrong day and the Manor was locked. On returning to Penfound, they told Mrs. Tucker how they had seen a young woman looking out of one of the upstairs windows. 'From up there,' they said, pointing to Kate's traditional window. "I tested them," Doris Tucker explained, "by pointing to another window and saying: 'Are you sure it wasn't this window?' But they stuck to their story. Two quite superior women, they could have been schoolmistresses, moreover, they insisted they knew nothing about the legend."

Kenneth Tucker recalled another woman. "She was of a party I was showing over the house; she was a very stout woman, and after we'd done our tour of the ground floor, she said she wouldn't come upstairs . . . her weight was too much and she didn't feel like dragging herself up the staircase. When I came downstairs again I found her, in very distressed condition, sitting in the porch." 'I couldn't remain inside,' she said. 'I'm a medium, and I feel this place is haunted . . . there's a terrible pain across my stomach . . . as if somebody had stabbed me.' "At first I thought she was putting it on, then she suddenly surprised me by asking" 'Did one of the old occupants have the name of Editha or something like that?' "I don't see how she could have known that the house was once owned by Queen Edith, and, of course, in *Domesday Book*, she's known as Queen Eddeva."

The Millses, also former residents of Penfound, writing to me from Bottreaux, Fort George, Guernsey, admitted they had had no "personal strange experiences" in their time at the Manor, but that a guest had seen "a figure of a girl standing at the foot of his bed."

Some weeks after my visit to Penfound Manor, I received further news of Kate Penfound. This time from Gladys Hopper, at Rosemont, a cottage near Dimma Chapel. Gladys Hopper's grandfather farmed the Penfound estate. "But my grandmother only kept her clothes in Kate's bedroom . . . nobody would sleep there. According to my mother, grandmother saw fleeting glimpses of a young lady. I don't think she would have said so if she hadn't seen something." Gladys Hopper also mentioned the Staceys who had once occupied the Manor. "I've heard it said both Mr. and Mrs. Stacey saw the figure of a young lady." This information confirmed something Kenneth Tucker had told me : "One of the visitors - it was about five years ago, I think - introduced himself as Mr. Stacey's son. He quite openly asked if we'd seen any ghosts and went on to say his father had seen Kate several times."

Tradition has it that Kate reappears punctually on the hour of midnight on the 26th of each April, when the sad ghostly climax is repeated in the courtyard. Other than April 26th, Kate is reputed periodically to pace a never-changing route. making her exit at the head of the main staircase. "We'd be glad to welcome Kate." said Kenneth Tucker, "but to date she has not shown herself on the anniversary or any other night."

Another theory has it that a tunnel or semi-underground passage once linked Penfound Manor and Poundstock Church, a matter of roughly a mile and a quarter. No trace though has been found in either the churchyard or the Manor, or in the Smugglers' Lane that runs alongside the former.

The Parish of Poundstock sprawls over four-thousand and seven-hundred acres, the approximate equivalent of thirteen square miles. This is contrasting country : cliffs of four-hundred feet measured against deep valleys like Trebarfoote Coombe and New Mills. In the east; hilly pastureland and sheltered lanes, dramatic seascapes and pastoral settings of cottages and gardens.

Built in a hollow and sheltered by elms, St. Neot's Church has the air of Anglo-Catholicism of the 1890's. Its west tower is crowned by pinnacles. On the north wall are frescoes depicting the Tree of Deadly Sin and Christ of the Trades. The nearby stone and cob Guildhouse, dating from the 15th century, is the only complete medieval guildhouse still in use in the county. During its lifetime it has served as Guild Hall, Poor House and Church Room.

St. Neot himself is worthy of a biography. A Celtic saint, belonging to the fifth or sixth century, he was reputed to be a brother of King Alfred and the founder of Oxford University. A dwarf-like figure, he spent hours in his favourite well, on the other side of Bodmin Moor, in meditation, and immersed to the neck. Many miracles have been attributed to his powers.

The church, which takes his name, has lived through tempestuous times. Three hostile famillies, the Bedruggans, the Bevilles and the Bloyous, all had conflicting interests in the parish of Poundstock, interests more materialistic than spiritual. One of the Bedruggans became rector but was excommunicated in 1261. Then, in 1282, the rector of Morwenstow allied himself to the Bloyous clan and drove the Poundstock priest out of his parish. An appeal went to Canterbury; Archbishop Peckham journeyed west and reinstated the lawful rector.

"The dark days of rebellion against Holy Church came to their tragic climax however, in 1357," wrote the Vicar of Poundstock, the Rev. P.R.F. Sanderson, in his handbook and guide. "William Penvoun (Penfound), the parish priest, a member of the Penfound family who supported the church, was now a target of bitter animosity and it needs little imagination beyond acquaintance with local surroundings to fill in the bare details of the crime. Whether or not he sensed that this morning, the Feast of St. John, would be his last on earth, the good man doubtless gave little heed as he left his cottage presbytery (now Dolebury) to walk down the leafy lane, over the little stream and up to the church door. 'Intoibo ad altare Dei' (I will go unto the altar of God) were the words on his lips. A little later, having sung Mass and greeted the faithful with 'Dominus vobiscum' (The Lord be with you) for the last time, rough voices shouted from outside above the howling gale. The door was thrown open, and the priest intercepted on his way from the altar by 'certain emissaries of Satan,' Parson Penvoun lay dead, robed in his Mass vestments, in a pool of life's blood on the chancel floor!"

The reason for my appearance at Poundstock early one November afternoon was a ghostly tradition. It is said the murdered priest occasionally reurns to the church.

I was particularly interested in one paragraph in the Rev. Sanderson's guide-book :

"... a parishioner entered the church and saw, as she thought, the vicar kneeling before the altar. Afterwards, as he made his way down the churchyard path, he was amazed to see the vicar descending down the path to the church from the top churchyard gate!"

Equipped with the name and address of the man who had witnessed the priest's reappearance, I arrived at a cottage with hope of solid confirmation. The alleged witness, I found doing some gardening for a neighbour. Instantly denying any such experience, he added : " The television people were around here, a while back asking me the same question . . . but I've seen no ghosts." I had however received a letter from a former parishioner, who told me how a certain woman, still resident in Poundstock, had seen the figure of the murdered Penfound only a few years ago. But again I met vehement denial : " Somebody's spreading rumours . . . and don't you put my name in any book!" Conversation at the Rectory revealed that the present incumbent has seen nothing either, but next day I travelled westward more hopefully.

At Cury Rectory, some four miles south of Helston, I met the Rev. Frederick William Marshall, who was born near Morwenstow and had been Vicar of Poundstock from 1945 to 1955. He is now responsible for both Cury and Gunwalloe. Compton Mackenzie spent part of his Cornish sojourn at Cury Rectory in the days of Father Sandys Wason. " The murder of the priest in the chancel wasn't the only tragedy at Poundstock " said the Rev. Marshall, sitting behind his desk. " There was the case of the Poundstock priest who was hanged for his part in the Pilgrimage of Grace." A smile crept across his face : " I remember at my induction at Poundstock the Bishop reminded the congregation what happened to their vicar when they didn't like him . . . perhaps he was giving them a bit of advice!"

" What about this ghost? Did you ever see him in your ministry at Poundstock?"

" More than once at Poundstock I was conscious of someone standing aside to let me go to the altar. I never saw anyone but I was definitely aware of someone stepping aside. Imagination? No, I don't think so. Of course, being a Celt I suppose I'm psychic!

" Actually, one of my Poundstock parishioners *did* see the murdered priest. One August, she went into church and saw me kneeling at the altar rail, preparing myself, as she thought, for confessions. I'm one of these characters who often go into the church an hour before the start of a service. She knew this, so she wasn't surprised to see me there. Time went by; she remained kneeling and the figure of the priest remained at the altar rail. She, kneeling further back in the church and preparing herself for confession, couldn't understand why I didn't make a move. Normally, I didn't keep people waiting long when they wanted to come to the confessional. But the minutes went by and nothing happened. Then, hearing movement and the sound of footsteps, she looked up in time to see the priest walking straight through the wall!"

The woman, who had experienced this appearance and disappearance of the ghost, no longer lived in Cornwall but, on obtaining her London address from Mr. Marshall, I wrote to her, asking for confirmation. Again denial : the third in three days. A fourth person alleged to have seen the ghost is an ex-schoolmistress, who had emigrated to New Zealand - unfortunately, in this instance, I could not trace her address. I did, in fact receive a fifth name : a deceased farmer. " A man of integrity" I was told, " and he definitely saw the ghost of the murdered priest." But as far as the living were concerned, I felt, at Poundstock, for the first time, I had run into collective opposition. Every enquiry, the Rev. Marshall excepted, was either denied or evaded.

Gunwalloe, the Rev. Marshall's second church, is a remote building hunched against a small, rocky headland : a beautiful, unexpected sight. No other church, throughout the length and breadth of ecclesiastical Cornwall, generates quite such an atmosphere. I have come several times and have never failed to catch the scent of its magic. Inevitably though a question stirs : " Why here?" Raison d'etre is difficult. The tower is, in fact, detached from the main building. Built against rock, it has two storeys with a pyramidal roof, and is older than the present church. There are two delightful but hopelessly improbable theories for this separation and selection of site. One is that two sisters, who were saved from a vessel on the rocks, resolved to build a church at Gunwalloe, but argued about the precise positioning - and compromised. A second theory is pure legend. The original intention, it is said, was to build the church in a more central place, but as fast as the builders' materials were brought to the chosen location, they were removed 'by some mysterious agency' to the cove.

" The glory of a building," wrote Ruskin, " is in its age, and in that deep sense of voicefulness, of stern watching, of mysterious sympathy, nay, even of approval or condemnation which we feel in walls that have been washed by waves of humanity." Such words apply to Gunwalloe. " The sea actually washes its walls " explained the vicar, " and the greatest waves fly over it!"

Below and beyond lies treasure. In 1526 the *St. Andrew*, carrying a valuable cargo for the King of Portugal, perished in a storm. Copper, silver, plate, precious stones, jewellery and chests crammed with coins, all disappeared beneath the sea. In

1785, another ship went down with another cargo of money. The beach here is a mixture of sand and large, rounded pebbles. To the left is the green carpet-like expanse of Mullion Golf Course and the Towans, high, grassy dunes, saved by the National Trust.

"I go down to Gunwalloe almost every day," the Rev. Marshall explained, "and very often I'm conscious of something deeply spiritual there. I've never seen anything, but I've many times felt surrounded by the departed. At service, when I say: 'The Lord be with thy spirit,' I get a response that goes beyond the number of those present. The odour of past prayer hangs about the place.

"Have you ever heard the story of the Cornish parson who called a service on the night of All Souls? Normally, he had a very regular, very faithful flock but, on this night of All Souls, not a person turned up. Later he found out why. They believed all the departed souls came to church that night. Those who had died without repenting were kept outside the churchyard gates and walls; those who had made a little amendment were allowed to go as far as the porch; and only those who had been Communicants were allowed inside. It's said to be a true story. I'm certainly conscious of the presence of others down at Gunwalloe."

BOSCASTLE 4

Witchcraft

"The most interesting and instructive work that could be written," reflected Dr. Johnson, "would be a History of Magic."

Witchcraft, undeniably fascinating, is a subject capable of arousing merely macabre curiosity or intense passion. Like hanging or hunting, abortion or euthanasia, it is a theme which attracts no neutrals.

In his *Encyclopedia of Witchcraft and Demonology,* Russell Hope Robbins, a Fellow of the Royal Society of Literature wrote: "The record of witchcraft is horrible and brutal: degradation stifled decency, the filthiest passions masqueraded under the cover of religion, and man's intellect was subverted to condone bestialities that even Swift's Yahoos would blush to commit. Never were so many so wrong, so long. Witchcraft destroyed the principles of honour and justice; it opened wide the rosters for the Hall of Shame . . . "

Who is a witch?

George Giffard, an eminent Elizabethan writer and theologian, understood the witch to be "one that worketh by the Devil, or by some devilish or curious art, either hurting or healing, revealing things secret, or foretelling things to come, which the Devil hath devised to entangle and snare men's souls withal to damnation. The conjuror, the enchanter, the sorcerer, the diviner, and whatsoever sort there is, are in deed encompased within this circle."

Witches and witchcraft, of course, mean different things to different people.

Of its nature and appeal, Lady Peirse has written:

"They may call it psychism or occultism; they may learn to cure or cast spells; they may invoke the help of the powers of evil, but it is practically the same thing, and its lure to mankind is as old and mysterious as the wind that blows over the earth, urging them with strange elusive thrills to recapture and use the old powers of the Serpent."

Though today we think of " witch " as automatically female, the word, in fact, derives from the old English masculine noun-substantive, *wicca* : " A man who practises witchcraft or magic ; a magician, sorcerer, wizard."

'The Great Beast,' Aleister Crowley visited Cornwall several times. Rough Tor on Bodmin Moor and the Hooting Carn down in the Hundred of Penwith have been mentioned as settings for Black Mass ceremonies. Cornwall's remoter regions like the wild, windswept moors certainly lend themselves in the eye of imagination to such ritual. Since the repeal in 1951 of the two-hundred and thirty-three year old Witchcraft Act, British witches, freed from the fear of legal prosecution, have been forming covens north, south, east and west. One practitioner believes there are nearly three thousand witches operating today.

Anyone, interested in the subject, would profit from a visit to Boscastle, that picturesque port high on the North Cornish coast. The River Valency slicing a deep glen, surges between buildings, meets the Jordan and is then swallowed by the sea. It is an unusual harbour : a medieval breakwater, a long, grey slipway and a huge rocky dog-leg opening into the ocean. Tucked inland and nearly out of sight of the sea, the harbour was created by constructing a mole or pier out into the channel, with a second one opposite. The way in is tortuous. Occasionally a boat has to be hauled in. Cliffs, of slate and shale tower impressively, somehow giving an impression of reluctance ; a reluctance to admit the Atlantic or let loose the Valency and the Jordan. Times were when Boscastle was a busy, bustling port dealing with one hundred ton vessels that were towed in by men rowing boats, aided by horses on the tow paths. Traffic was two-way : boats bringing in coal from Northumberland and taking away Cornish minerals and slate.

Boscastle is, in fact, the Castle Boterel in Thomas Hardy's novel *A Pair of Blue Eyes*, the story of a young architect coming to North Cornwall in connection with a church restoration (as Hardy actually did at nearby St. Juliot) a story of romance that ends in tragedy with the two lovers travelling on the same train, one a corpse inside a coffin.

Close by the water's edge is the Witch's House. Formerly a mineral store and a shipping warehouse, this old stone building has been transformed into a witchcraft museum. Its proprietor is Devonshire-born Cecil Hugh Williamson, who lives down on the south coast at Polperro.

"I was in films, worked way back in the silent days, which will give you some idea of my age . . . in those days, before the unions, you did a bit of everything - camera assistant, lighting, a bit of acting, the lot really. Later I did some documentaries, including some on supernatural subjects. I've always been interested in the supernatural."

We talked in the box office. Admission prices were on the wall. I sat in an armchair. Bespectacled, Cecil Williamson, casually dressed in cravat, sweater and grey slacks, sat opposite me, perched on a stool, his left arm resting on the box office counter. An electric fire took some of the chill from a cold, wet afternoon. Rain muttered on the roof. To my right were a sculpted figure of Meg Morrilles, a stuffed bat, mortar and pestle. To the left a tea pot; the statuette of a cat and a puffer fish.

"Oh, yes, there are witches in Cornwall, but there are musicians and mathematicians, too. A matter of the law of averages really, you'll find some witches in almost every society, not many, just a few . . . No, I wouldn't introduce you to a witch. I'd be introducing you to a law-breaker and possibly a murderer. These people have no scruples. They'll kill if necessary. If somebody wants a person out of the way, and the witch's help is given, people *are* eliminated. An elderly person may be obstructing an inheritance while they live; the person wanting the money has to go without . . . and that's where, when and why the witch's help is sometimes asked for. I'm not joking. The deeper you go into witchcraft, the more sinister it becomes.

"There are basically four aspects of magical operation. First, you have the source of the elemental spirit force; secondly, you have the witch; thirdly, you have the client; and fourthly, the objective. A lot of witches are part-timers - by that I mean, they have a profession or business and the witchcraft is only part of their life, admittedly they'd say an important part. Witchcraft's a very private, very personal service. Each case calls for considerable expenditure of time and energy. It also involves considerable expenditure in the other sense. A witch expects payment; on occasions very big sums of money pass hands. The rituals themselves are elaborate, long incantations, a secret language is spoken: a mumbo-jumbo of gibberish sounds . . . ill-wishing's principally through a powerful form of prayer, a projecting of thoughts to the exclusion of all else throughout the operation. While there's hate, envy, greed, lust and jealousy in the world, the witch won't be short of clients."

"Are you a witch?" I asked, wondering if such a question might bring our interview to an abrupt end.

David Waddon-Martyn: "Since having gone through these experiences . . . I do believe in the supernatural." Chapter 1

Cleave Camp: "... high on the cliffs of North Cornwall ... might have been lifted from the set of a Hitchcock film ... there was no stopping the mysterious nightly bombardment ..." Chapter 2

Penfound Manor: ". . . an idyllic old English home that belonged to an ancient family of the same name." Chapter 3

Kate's Bedroom: ". . . nobody would sleep there . . . fleeting glimpses of a young lady."
Chapter 3

Cecil Williamson smiled, then laughed: "No, I'm not a witch in your sense of the word. You can call me an occultist, a demonologist, if you wish. I don't belong to any group or society; very much an individualist really. Aleister Crowley once advised me to steer clear of cult groups inside witchcraft. If you don't, you run into trouble; you're identified as one of a certain sect and the others look on you as an enemy or nuts. I've delved into the subject and have gathered a mass of information over the last twenty-five years. Who knows what I shall do with it? Most likely I shall destroy it, unless someone can convince me of a worthwhile reason for its preservation or publication.

"How does one become a witch? Any qualification, any form of examination?"

"In my experience, and in spite of what the Sunday papers say, there are no schools for graduate witches. Like musicians, sculptors, writers, steeplejacks, the person has a natural inclination to occult matters. They become immersed in the subject, and if they are to succeed, they start to work acts of witchcraft. If they're any good, they will soon get proof of their powers by the success of their operations. This is as if it were fuel to their fire of belief . . . they go on, step by step, gaining confidence and faith in their power to work magic. Soon the word spreads and they draw to themselves other workers in the field of magic. Information is exchanged - know how - and, most important, they form a bond whereby one will help the other. In this way a mutual friendship chain can be built up, joining, link by link, across the country. For example, a Cornish witch of my knowledge reached through eighteen persons, by using word of mouth from Cornwall to Cambridge, and she'd never met or spoken to fifteen of them; but the Cambridge-sited witch did what she was asked to do in Cambridge for her unseen sister witch in Cornwall.

"Mark you, there are many basic principles which are common the world over, so it is that the methods and materials are geared to the operation on hand. The operation dictates the group of instruments and materials to be used. Their numbers are large, so it is up to the witch to make the selection that suits her methods. For example, if death is to play a part in the work, then black instruments are used; blood, too, bones from dead humans or animals, maybe flies, worms and decayed materials of all sorts. A small animal like a mouse, a bird or a snake may be slowly killed by being starved to death. So the point is, no matter where you are in the world, either today or in the remote past, one can soon identify what the aim of the operation is by getting a sight of the materials used.

" There are very few covens or groups in the popular sense. Most witches work alone or in twos and threes, and remember, not one of them - if a true witch - will do anything for nothing; they are in a trade like anybody else, and they insist on payment for goods and services, but, unlike most High Street traders, they do not have bad debts. No one can be that stupid, for the first attribute of a worthwhile witch is that she dispenses with heart and feeling. A witch has no heart. That she sold to the Devil the day she became convinced of her supernatural powers. That act she does on her own, of her own free wish, much in the same way that a person, taken with religion, will say that the spirit of the Lord fell upon him and entered into his body. There is, indeed such a thing as 'The Thrill of Evil.' It's far more exciting than drugs, drink or sex."

Here, at Boscastle, there is much to whet the witchcraft appetite : grotesque headmasks, a belt worn by the Moon Maiden in rituals, a bottle of witch's brew, which is, in fact, a delicious Italian liqueur; the skin of a snake, used as the warlock's belt or the witch's garter; two witches' trumpets made from human thigh bones, used for calling up the spirits of the dead in acts of Necromancy; instruments of African witch doctors; photographs and engravings, depicting various aspects of the craft, including bare-breasted women and well-known white witches; a model of the famous Plymouth chair, made just over the Tamar and shipped across the Atlantic for witch burning. These were only a handful of the exhibits. Piece de resistance though was the skeleton of Ursula Kemp, the witch of St. Osyth, Essex, whose bones lie in an open elm coffin upon royal purple satin. Cecil Williamson's removal of the body from its grave, at a building site in the High Street of St. Osyth was filmed on Anglia Television. " I discovered that iron spikes had been driven through her body to hold her down in the grave, and to prevent her from haunting the parish." Some of the iron spikes were on display alongside the coffin.

A less dramatic exhibit, but one which still fascinated me, was a green glass bottle, " compounded by a West Cornwall Wise Woman, working in the Ludgvan area, containing a mixture of seven herbs, human hair, shadow dirt, pins and various magical powers. It was never used. The intended victim died in a road accident."

" How would such a concoction be used by the witch?" I asked.

" Normally, by digging a hole in the ground, probably in the middle of a field. The wise woman might also pee into the hole, then, naked, dash round the border of the field seven times . . .

this would happen at night, you'll understand, when nobody's around . . . ill wishing some person or some disease that may be in the soil, and then, ritual over, she'd probably hop aboard her moped and ride home . . . dressed, of course.

"I can appreciate your difficulties," Cecil Williamson continued, "writing about Black Magic isn't easy, so much is secret . . . and anyway, if you know about a murder, the police will want to know about it, too! There was the case of one writer who made certain revelations; the witches got hold of this and threatened him; the police got hold of it, too, and brought him to court. In the end, he had to stand up and say he'd invented it all. He was standing to lose either way; put behind bars or got at by the witches. He retracted, and was fined £50 for being a public nuisance!

"Now perhaps you'll see why I said I wouldn't introduce you to a witch. I remember, a few years ago, a journalist did a series of articles on witchcraft for one of the Sunday newspapers . . . he'd promised to take the lid off witchcraft . . . anyway, after the series had appeared he went on the continent for a holiday, and how he survived a most terrible motoring accident there was a miracle . . ."

"You're quite serious about witches setting out to finish off people?"

"Absolutely. I knew a case of one man who, after a witch had got to work on him, became accident prone. In the end, one day, on the road, attempting to avoid one car, he went under the wheels of another . . . it's a subtle process."

ST. NECTAN'S GLEN 5

Hermitage & Waterfall

Once more I returned to the corkscrewing A 39 - but a place nearer home this time.

St. Nectan's Glen is on the landward side of the Boscastle to Tintagel road, between Trethevy and Bossiney. On sheet 174 of the Ordnance Survey map, it is less than an inch of green near a quarry and a burial chamber. In reality it is one of the most beautiful corners of North Cornwall. " Full of poetry and coloured by legend " said Robert Hunt more than seventy years ago, . . . many a spot of quiet beauty solicits you to loiter, and loitering you feel that there are places from which the winds gather poetry."

There are various approaches. The easiest is from the lane beyond the Rocky Valley Hotel. Red arrows on trees in the glen indicate the way. Pilgrims used the same route in the sixth century when they came to pray at the shrine of St. Nectan. Some say the Saint, from his tower, could see the coast and Tintagel Castle and that he rang a silver bell, warning sailors of submerged rocks.

Numerous are the stories concerning St. Nectan, the hermitage and the glen that took his name. A writer, who lived nearby, claimed that he often heard the chanting of monks at night. A workman at Bossiney House told me how one evening on hearing invisible sobbing in the glen he had stopped to investigate - only to be mocked by weird, inexplicable laughter. Kathleen Everard, a neighbour, talked of beautiful organ music coming from an empty building.

I first explored the glen in spring when it lay in a blend of sunshine and shadow. Bluebells splashed their colour over a green treed landscape. Shadows were stretching and everywhere one was conscious of spring stirring. The glen is surrounded by trees; trees of seemingly a thousand and one shapes. Some straight as telegraph poles, others like drunken exclamation marks with branches bent beyond the imagination of a human sculptor.

At the head of the glen is The Hermitage, believed to be the site of the Saint's cell. Today it has become The Hermitage Tea Gardens. For a small fee, you may descend twisting steps, stand on duckboards and watch one of the finest sights in the whole county : a waterfall that thunders through a natural arch, plunges over a stone obstacle, falls forty feet and then races away down the glen. Further down, this water divides Rocky Valley, passing a ruined mill and mysterious, ancient rock engravings, before becoming a mere drop in the ocean.

I still remember my first visit and the impression : spray, lit by sunlight, rising like some strange incantations. The realization that most legends are only good stories and yet, retaining a *feeling* that *something* happened here.

Local tradition maintains that when St. Nectan died, two ladies, thought to be his sisters, (a distinct possibility, for there were twenty-four children) took possession of the chapel and, according to the Saint's wishes, buried him with his sacramental vessels and treasure in an oak chest. Diverting the waters of the fall, they dug a grave in the river bed below the kieve, which in our Cornish language means basin, and buried the chest. Whereupon the river turned back on to its natural course and flowed over the Saint's grave. The sisters remained at the chapel, leading remote lives, existing on an austere diet of wild berries, fresh fruit and raw fish. They were thought to be agents of the Devil and were blamed for any calamities. If a cow or a sheep became ill, the sisters were accused. One sister died and the other mourned to the extent that she too, passed away. Buried together, they are said to lie beneath a flat stone in the glen and their spirits are reputed to haunt Genver Lane.

In 1966 I wrote an article on the waterfall and glen for *The Cornish Magazine*, concluding with a question to the then occupant, Mrs. Thompson.

" Have you personally had any strange experiences here ?" I asked her.

" Well, at nights," she replied, " we sometimes hear strange noises . . . we let the dogs out but they only go as far as the gate, and there they stand howling terribly . . . One night I did see a woman . . . a complete stranger . . . here inside the building. My husband said it was just my imagination, but it wasn't . . . "

Shortly after its publication, Mrs. Thompson telephoned me to say her husband, an absolute sceptic on supernatural possibility, had now changed his mind. Twice, in quick succession, he had seen the figure of a stranger in the private grounds. Twice the figure had unaccountably vanished. Unfortunately, by the time

I had begun collecting material for this book, the Thompsons had left St. Nectan's Glen and I have since been unable to renew contact.

Conversation with Peggy Garside, a neighbour at Bossiney, however revealed some fresh evidence. Peggy, who had acted in some of the earliest productions at the Minack Theatre, near Land's End, and I were discussing various beauty spots, when she confessed: "I haven't been to the glen for about twenty years." She and a friend had walked to the waterfall but neither exchanged a word until they were out of the glen once more. "Did you see him?" asked Peggy. "Yes," replied her friend, "he was in grey." They had both been conscious of a ghostly, monk-like figure following them. The next day I wrote to the friend, Maud Hudson, who lives at Higher Compton, Plymouth. "Peggy is quite right," she replied, "We saw the figure dressed in grey with a blue lining to the hood . . . he was very kind-looking, and though unnerving, I did not feel afraid . . ."

Mary Bowley, who lives in Dorset, but is a frequent visitor to Tintagel, added another interesting strand. "There was an army officer; he'd just arrived in the district - the first day of his holiday. Before dinner, he decided to take a stroll up the glen. Over dinner he remarked: 'By the way, I didn't know you had a monastery here.' 'A monastery?' somebody asked curiously. 'Why yes, I met three monks in the glen . . . all cheerful fellows!' The soldier later declared he knew nothing of the legends."

I asked more recent occupants of The Hermitage if they had seen or heard anything unusual.

"I'm not a convinced disciple of the supernatural" Peter Hawthorn admitted, "but when we first came, I was interested in the behaviour of our two Siamese cats. In Genver Lane they behaved very strangely, lashing out at an invisible opponent, almost boxing, standing on their hind legs, as if up against somebody or something a little bigger than themselves. Personally, I've seen or heard nothing out of the ordinary. The fascinating thing to me is, how this valley picks up sound. The top part of the valley is like a thumping great ear-drum." His wife Wendy has not seen anything remotely supernatural, either. "But in the orchard you sometimes get a feeling that you're not alone . . . and on several occasions I've distinctly heard footsteps, but on checking, have found nobody there . . ."

Those were the Hawthorns' replies on first meeting, but later, on a return to The Hermitage, I encountered a different response.

“Something’s happened since your last visit” Wendy Hawthorn explained. Taking me to a spot just above The Hermitage and close to the stream she told me how early one evening she and her husband had seen a figure walking across a tangled piece of vegetation towards the water. Treading the route carefully, she halted by a sweet chestnut: “At this point, the figure just vanished. I remember it was tall, donkey grey in colour and hooded. At first, we thought it was one of the neighbours. But it simply vanished . . . no trace anywhere, either on the ground or in the stream.”

“Was it perhaps a shadow or a trick of the light?”

Peter Hawthorn was emphatic. “The sun had set, no question of a shadow . . . a very definite form . . . a man I’d say judging by his stature and gait. The intriguing thing was the pace he moved at. He was travelling across brambles and undergrowth; the average person would have moved carefully, slowly, yet this figure moved rapidly like a man walking along a smooth path or road or alternatively, a piece of ground he knew well. He was travelling in the direction of the old clapper bridge. There was no question of his hiding behind the tree, we explored the whole area. I’ve thought of all the logical explanations but there just isn’t one.”

BOSSINEY 6

Midsummer Eve Lights

King Arthur has grown into a bone of bitter controversy. Historians have been arguing for years : " Did Arthur reign in reality or fantasy?" The Welsh and the Scots, the French and the German, not to mention men of Somerset, have all claimed him.

Arthur, if he really existed, belonged to the Dark Ages; somewhere between the arrival of the English in 499 and the Normans in 1066. The infiltration of the West was resolutely opposed under, we believe, the inspiring leadership of a chieftain, probably a kind of guerilla fighter. Was it Arthur? Or did Arthur grow out of his deeds?

Legend tells us Tintagel was Arthur's birth place. One account says he was washed ashore, as a babe, close to Merlin's Cave, just below the castle. Another says he was born of a magical union between Uther Pendragon, High King of England, and Igerne, wife of Gorlois, Duke of Cornwall.

My own supernatural encounter was Arthurian in origin. When it happened though, in 1965, I made no special claims, read no Arthurian significance into the situation. I merely accepted that something out of the ordinary had occurred, kept strictly to the *facts* and left interpretations to others. I still maintain that policy.

It happened almost on our doorstep, for Bossiney Mound is no more than two-hundred yards from Bossiney House. Alongside the hotel is the local chapel, and just off is the road that connects Tintagel and Boscastle, it is neither a particularly photogenic subject nor a landmark likely to excite the average tourist. Gorse, ash, brambles, hemlock, cocksfoot and bracken are some of the ingredients which clothe this hump.

Legend has it that King Arthur's round table lies buried beneath the mound, and that it comes to the surface one night a year in shimmering silver. Midnight on Midsummer Eve, they say is the time to see this spectacle.

It was Midsummer Eve, 1965, and my first summer in Tintagel. I was listening to the radio - *A Book at Bedtime* had just ended. Was it worth staying up? A few days ago I had resolved to visit the Mound at the appointed hour and put legend to test. "The Mound's no great distance away" I told myself. "Of course you won't see anything but you will, at least, have given the dog and yourself some exercise!" Hands on the clock stood at twenty minutes to midnight as I put Tex on to his lead. Down in the hall a surprise awaited me: three hotel guests greeted my emergence.

"May we please come with you to the Mound?"

Earlier in the evening I had told their party of six about the legend. The other three had gone to bed.

"Certainly."

But in all honesty I was annoyed. This was something I had wanted to do alone. As far as human companions were concerned, I wanted none. Their presence irritated. Moreover, I felt oddly embarrassed as we walked across the gravelled forecourt. "You're a fool" an inner voice said. "You're leading these people up the garden path. They're doomed to disappointment." As we strolled along the road, I started making some sort of apology, preparing them from the inevitable anti-climax. "These legends are very interesting but nothing really happens," I warned them. Soon the murky shapes of Bossiney Mound and the Chapel loomed up in front of us. There was no hint of a moon, the wind sent the slightest of shivers through the darkness. Personally, I felt refreshed, very awake and yet, the presence of the trio still gnawed.

At the end of Bossiney Lane I left the others, who planned to take a closer look at the Mound and Chapel, while I took Tex for a run. We agreed to link up a few minutes before midnight. Freed from his lead, Tex bounded away down the bumpy lane; a loose television aerial rattled, the sea's volume increased as we moved on in the direction of the cliffs. A light in one of the bungalows went out; now there was only darkness, save the pale beam of my torch.

It was shortly after ten to twelve when I got back to the top of the lane. There was no sign of the others; I guessed them to be somewhere near the Chapel. I looked towards the Mound.

Would the table appear tonight?

Of course it wouldn't.

I thought of Sir Francis Drake standing there. Until the Reform Bill of 1832, Bossiney, with sister Trevena, returned two Members of Parliament. There on Castle Hill, as it was called, Cornishmen raised their hands to send the conqueror of the Armada to Westminster. There too, Bristol traders brought their slaves and auctioned them to the gentry.

Historical reflection however, was rudely shattered, for a light suddenly appeared inside one of the chapel windows. It grew - a glow rather than a single shaft of electricity, like a patch of floodlit moorland mist. Soon it covered both windows.

How long did the light shine ?

I honestly don't know ! A minute, perhaps two. I recall no sense of fear, for it held me fascinated. When the light went out, I started searching for explanations. A reflection ? I studied the windows of the houses opposite. They stood silent and dark : a negative reply to my unspoken question. Only one house in the entire vicinity revealed a light, and I knew it had no connection with the glow from within the chapel. A passing car perhaps ? But I recalled no traffic.

Three frightened figures hurried towards me from the little side road that climbs to Camelford or Launceston.

"Did you see that light ?" they asked.

"Yes," I replied.

"So did we - we were right by the Chapel. We saw it come on and then go out."

"It was like a mist spreading, more than a light said a second voice.

"And did you see it ?" I asked the third and youngest member of the party.

"No," she confessed, "I was too frightened to look !"

We walked down to the Chapel. I was keen to make a closer inspection of the building. Conceivably, somebody inside had turned on a light. The Chapel though, showed no sign of light or life. A tiny couryard separates the road and the chapel door. I apprcached the entrance, but Tex, now back on his lead, refused to go near the entrance. Normally a pugnacious animal, he suddenly seemed a coward ; he tugged violently in the other direction. I coaxed and slowly he came, grudgingly.

I tried the door. But it was bolted.

"Anybody there ?" I called out hopefully but there was no reply.

We got back to the main Tintagel-Boscastle road ; peered at the Chapel windows again, and then at the Mound. Only darkness stared back.

Slowly, reluctantly, we walked up the road in the direction of Bossiney House.

"The others'll never believe us," said the young man.

"I don't care what they think or say," retorted the other witness, " we *know* we saw something. I'll always believe it was something to do with the legend. Why tonight ? And why so near the Mound ?"

After breakfast next morning, the mystery deepened. Another inspection of the Chapel revealed that the windows, from which the light had appeared, were covered by blinds.

That same afternoon, I was shown over this Bible Christian place of worship by Jack Dymond, a retired farmer who was then our gardener at Bossiney House. One of the Chapel's trustees, he had been baptised here in 1896. "And," he added " I've been connected with the place ever since."

I told him about the light and asked about the blinds.

" Well, all I can tell you is, they've been down since Sunday evening's service."

We were standing in the blue carpeted aisle which leads to the Communion Table and Pulpit. Eight rows of pews stretched from wall to wall ; in one corner stood the organ.

" Do you think anybody came in last night and switched on the light ?" I enquired.

" Nobody was inside the place."

" Could the light have been reflected from the other side of the chapel ?"

We looked through the second pair of windows to the adjoining Methodist property.

" Impossible, I'd say. There was nobody in there either."

" How do you explain this strange light, then Jack ?"

'You can't . . . you must accept it . . . man doesn't know everything . . ."

To the puzzlement of friends I have not attempted a return visit on the anniversary. Other people have gone there on the stroke of midnight, but they have seen or heard nothing beyond the normal. Perhaps the knowledge that others were going to be there deterred me. Perhaps I am simply afraid of disappointment. I have since though, seen reflections in the chapel windows. Reflections of street lights, which bore no resemblence to the glow of that Midsummer Eve.

In retrospect, most significant of all was the behaviour of Tex, a sensitive little animal, he was particularly so in his response to atmosphere, places or people. I remember setting out early one September morning with photographer friend, Bryan Russell, for Rough Tor and Brown Willy. I took my notebook ; Bryan his cameras. We intended to do an article on the two hills for *The Cornish Magazine*, entitled *On the Roof of Cornwall.* Tex came with us and ruined the whole expedition. The higher we went, the more apprehensive he became. Tail down, eyes mirroring first distrust, and then something akin to fear, he made a forlorn figure. On top of Rough Tor, Bryan got to work with his camera and I made some notes ; but Tex hid in a crevice. Brown Willy, on the other side of the valley, had a majestic, beckoning quality that morning, as sunlight rimmed the skyline and the haze dissolved. Yet Tex was not to be enticed. He refused to go another inch, instead he shook like a seriously-ill animal. His condition was such that I called off the second leg of the journey and immediately started the descent back to Rough Tor Farm and the car. Disappointment over not making Brown Willy, our premier goal, was overshadowed by my concern for Tex. I was already contemplating breaking our journey at Camelford and visiting the Veterinary Surgeon. For once, Tex was happy to be carried : a four-legged parcel of tension. Halfway down the slope however, he began struggling for his feet. I gently placed him on the ground and he scampered away : a different dog. Something high up on the roof of Cornwall had disturbed him. Neither Bryan nor myself had a clue. Even today, we are none the wiser. Did his animal instinct detect something beyond our vision and comprehension ?

There have been other instances too. I once visited a house where a murder had been committed ; spending some time in fact, in the room where the deed had been perpetrated. Tex came with me. Personally I found it a perfectly normal bedroom, in a perfectly normal house. But Tex was a bundle of agitation - whining and moving anxiously from room to room. Anxious to leave, he only settled again, when he jumped into the back of the car and I drove off.

There is a delightful walk from Bossiney House to Barras Head, site of an earthworks far older than Tintagel Castle and the first piece of land to be bought by the National Trust outside Wales. A path snakes it way along the cliffs and out to the headland. Barras Nose as local people call it and, at one point, Tex always halted. Nothing would induce him to go on, not even the bribery of a biscuit. " Foxes " somebody said. But I was less sure, for the pattern persisted during all four seasons. At this particular point, the terrier willingly allowed me to carry him for something like ten yards, then he would struggle to continue on his own. On every return journey, he repeated the same performance, always halting at precisely the same spot.

TINTAGEL 7

Charmer

John of Ardene (1307-90) scholar and surgeon, and distinguished practitioner of medieval medicine, mentioned the employment of charms: "The words Melchior, Jasper and Balthazar to be written in blood from the little finger of the patient" as a cure for epilepsy. Folk medicine, in fact, occupies an important place in the background story and development of medicine. Douglas Gutherie, in his *A History of Medicine*, considered it worthy of study in any analysis of the subject: "Who has not met some friend who keeps his rheumatism in check by carrying in his pocket a raw potato or the right forefoot of a hare? Belief in such mascots is almost universal. The skin of a snake, the patella of a sheep, the nail of a coffin and all manner of other charms have been, and still are, in daily use." Gutherie wrote those words as recently as 1945.

In times past, charmers - sometimes called white witches - were called upon to offer protection against the spells of Black Magic. I heard of a case in Cornwall, where a woman asked a vicar for water from the font following a baptism, with the explanation that she needed holy water to undo a spell. Many are the stories of Cornish charmers.

But today however, charmers are few and far apart. As long ago as 1881, Robert Hunt was told there were only three charmers in the whole of West Cornwall. In Tintagel though we have one such practitioner. Charlie Bennett was born more than seventy years ago at Halgabron, a hamlet above Bossiney, on the road to Launceston. After a lifetime spent on the land, Charlie Bennett now enjoys an active retirement. Active on two scores: he still charms and he belongs to that disappearing race of hedge and wall builders. I have watched him, in his beret and shirt sleeves, turning slates and stones into a work of art. He has too, an individual trademark. If, in or around Tintagel, you find a wall or hedge containing a solitary brick, you can be certain Charlie Bennett was the man who built it. "Who knows, somebody, in fifty or a hundred years' time, may stop one day and ask themselves : 'Why did he put a brick there ? Was he short of a stone ?' It's a kind of little joke really. Not a bad thing to make people stop and think . . . is it ?"

There are numerous people in North Cornwall grateful for Charlie Bennett's healing gifts. Typical is the response of Charles Ferrett who only lives a cricketer's throw away from the charmer's house. "Because of an accident, I had to have a course of injections for my left hand, and about a dozen warts appeared. I went along to see Mr. Bennett. He just asked me my name, and within a few weeks they were all gone." William Bickle, a former neighbour, also told me how Charlie Bennett had wrought a cure without even seeing the patient. Through the course of business, William Bickle met a young man, needing help, in another area of North Cornwall. On being given the young man's full name and address, Charlie Bennett assured that the distant patient would lose his warts. "Within three weeks they'd disappeared." Farmers too are generous in their praise. In the words of one who farms in this district : "I can guarantee Charlie Bennett's powers. To begin with, I was a bit sceptical, but all the farmers around have talked about his powers . . . so I asked him to look at some bullocks of mine that had ring worm. They were cured ; I'm not cynical now. One can't understand it but that doesn't matter . . . the animals are cured and that's what matters."

A canary, Guy by name, sang in its cage as Charlie Bennett and I talked before a blazing, crackling fire at his home, 23 The Butts. "These houses are built on what used to be the old football field," said Charlie. Beyond the garden at the rear, Tintagel AFC's present pitch stretched across a gentle slope. Outside it was a cold, brilliantly sunlit morning. Frost was rapidly vanishing and ice was turning back to water.

"How did you begin charming ?" I asked "was it a family thing ?"

"In a way, yes. My mother and father both did a bit of charming. My mother cured sprains and thorn prickles and my father did ring worm and snake or adder bites. But charming for me really started forty years ago, when my daughter Barbara, then a little child, had ring worm. My brother, who was a charmer, tried to clear it up and so did a farmer, who was a charmer ; but the ring worm stayed. It was a ghastly thing ; big as the top of a tea cup, a horrible, big juicy one it was, on her face. So in the end I decided to have a go. I had this charm written down . . . never knew to this day who wrote it . . .but it worked. Within a couple of days it had begun to improve, and inside the month it was gone. I suppose the word got around after that and people started coming to me—they've kept coming ever since.

I'm usually busiest in the summer, when the visitors are about. Sometimes two or three people will turn up on the same day. No, I never take a penny. If somebody asks 'How much?' I say, you can put something in the blind box, mister, and how much you put in, is up to you . . ."

"The name of the patient's important, isn't it?"

"Oh, yes. Usually I ask them two questions. First, their full name, christian name and surname; then their age. Some of the ladies are a bit bashful about that, of course." he added, eyes twinkling as his face creased into a smile.

"I'm not asking you to give away secrets but the charm is a form of silent prayer, isn't it?"

Charlie looked pensive for a few moments. "You could put it that way. 'In the name of the Father, the Son and the Holy Ghost.' I usually end up with those words. But there's no pleading with God to cure this poor person. I'm doing it; I'm not asking God, but it's not my own power. Where does the power come from? Honestly, I don't know—I just don't know. And, when I'm charming, I get the feeling that I'm doing a kindness . . . nothing more . . . no electrical feeling in the nerves, no sense of having a special responsibility. I'm glad, of course, when a wart's clean gone."

"What's the actual pattern of charming?"

"Well, it may vary from charmer to charmer, but as far as I'm concerned, after I've asked those two questions about name and age, I circle my finger over the infected spot, travelling opposite to the way of the sun. What I say is said in silence, and it's all over in a matter of seconds. I charm ring worm in human beings and cattle and horses; warts too. I've never had the chance to draw out a snake or adder bite but I'm convinced I could do it. With cattle, I just walk around the single bullock and do that animal separately, quarter by quarter really, and you normally see a vast difference inside a week."

"What about failures?"

"Well I suppose there must be times when the charm doesn't work, but not many. Some people never come back to you, so you don't know whether they're cured or not. As I say, a lot of them come from away. Two years ago a man brought his stepson to me. The boy had a wart as big as a pea, a black one. They were going back to Bradford next day. Last summer they came back to Tintagel. 'How about that wart?' I asked. 'It fell off next day!' they told me. Then, some time ago, a man turned up at the gate and said: 'Mr. Bennett, you charmed my

Rev. F. W. Marshall: "More than once at Poundstock I was conscious of someone standing aside to let me go to the altar." Chapter 3

Interior of Poundstock Church:
". . . rough voices shouted from outside . . . the door was thrown open, and the priest intercepted on his way from the altar . . . Parson Penvoun, lay dead robed in his Mass vestments, in a pool of life's blood on the chancel floor!" Chapter 3

Cecil Williamson at his Boscastle Witchcraft Museum:
"You can call me an occultist, a demonologist, if you wish . . . Aleister Crowley once advised me to steer clear of cult groups inside witchcraft." Chapter 4

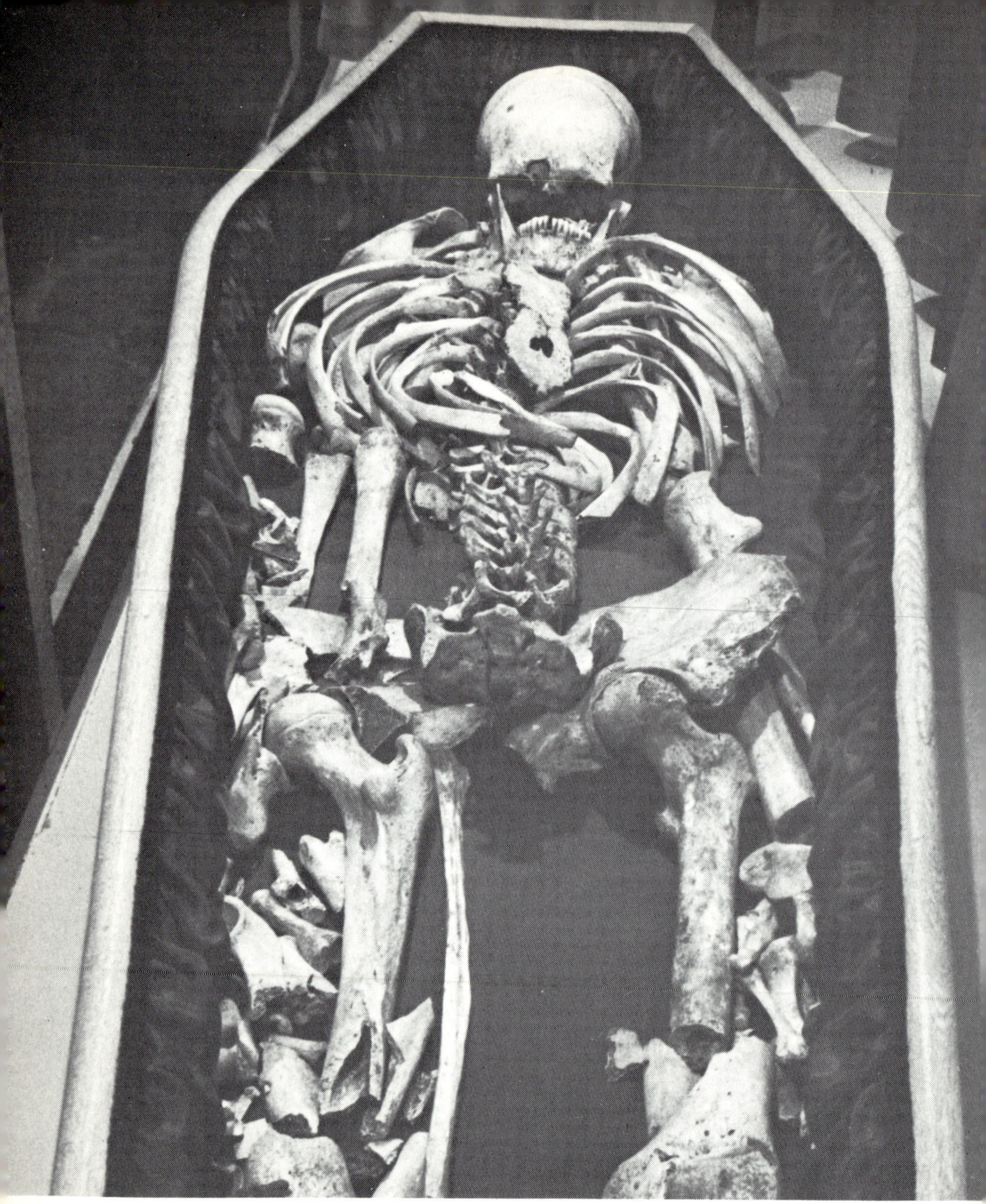

Skeleton of the Witch Ursula Kemp:
"spikes had been driven through her body to hold her down in the grave, and to prevent her from haunting the parish." Chapter 4

wart seven years ago and it did the trick. I know you shouldn't thank a charmer, but I'm thanking you - I don't think it'll come back now!' Some people saw me, of course, when I was on television with Polly Elwes, and when they're down in Cornwall - if they've some trouble - they come and see me. Never saw myself on television that night though - didn't know I was on!"

ST. AUSTELL 8

Spiritual Healer

That conversation with Charlie Bennett suddenly altered the character and the direction of my supernatural trail across Cornwall. My interest deepening, I began probing the realm of spiritual healing. * From Tintagel my route veered inland to St. Austell.

Saint Austell is a mystery, as vague as the Cornish landscape itself when insidious mist descends. Historians have searched but nobody has succeeded in tracing him.

Until the birth of the china clay industry, St. Austell was merely a village ; as the industry expanded, so St. Austell grew in size, in population and importance. Today St. Austell is the nerve-centre, the administrative headquarters of the industry. Out of Cookworthy's discovery, a unique terrain has emerged. The countryside, northward, is studded with mines or quarries. They are open to the sky these depths from which the clay is won. Huge white spoil heaps serrate the skyline. Milky green lakes lie in the shadow of the white cones. " This is the lunar and the lunatic landscape of the moon " Charles Causley has said " a weird, white world, dusted over with the colour of sex, where workers are like walking wedding cakes."

Two-hundred and forty-two miles from London, twenty from Liskeard and fourteen from Truro, St. Austell sprawls upon the A390. The town itself is something of a disappointment in that there is only a handful of notable old buildings : the Quaker Meeting House, the Market House, The White Hart Hotel (which still boasts a wallpaper, dating from 1800, depicting The Bay of Naples) but most imposing of all is the parish church of The Holy Trinity. Fragments of an earlier Norman building remain. The tower is a splendid, memorable construction. Battlemented and pinnacled, the west face is an arrangement of niches

*Turning to *The Concise Oxford Dictionary* I found the word " Supernatural " defined as " due to or manifesting some agency above the forces of nature, outside the ordinary operation of cause and effect " so on the strength of this definition, I have had no inhibitions about including spiritual healing under the supernatural umbrella.

with statues ; at the apex is a figure of God the Father holding a cross bearing God the Son.

My precise destination was Trevarthian Road, a sloping thoroughfare above the railway station. Light was fast ebbing from the sky and I was already using sidelights as I brought the car to a halt outside number twenty-four. Below the brewery and the football ground - almost next door to the Ministry of Labour, the words " Starclock Repairs " were written in white letters against a brown background above the shopwindow. " Are you afraid of Death or Dying ?" asked a notice in the window. I rang the bell and as lights appeared, on a yellowed newspaper cutting, I read : " Peter Sellars talks to dead mother - She knew I had her ring in my pocket."

Twenty-four Trevarthian Road is really three places in one. In the shop at the front, Alan Nance practises watchmaking and repairs, something he's been doing for roughly forty years. Timepieces of various types and qualities tick away, literally dozens of them. Beyond the shop is a small white painted lobby, where Alan Nance practises something quite different : spiritual healing. The next person to walk into the shop is more likely to ask for a healing than a watch repair. At the top of the stairs is a neatly arranged little flat, Alan Nance's home, where we talked, first in formal question and answer interview and later over the Cornish pasties he had just cooked, followed by apple pie and Cornish cream.

Alan Henry William Nance is a Scillonian. William Borlase, in his *Observations on the Ancient and Present State of the Isles of Scilly,* written in 1756, made reference to the Nance family : " The art of making kelp was never known in these Islands till introduced by Mr. Nance in 1684, as I was informed by his son, then eighty years of age, living in St. Martins who came over from Cornwall with his father (who is still remembered with gratitude) for the very purpose of carrying on the kelp manufacture, and has lived there ever since."

The Scillies lie twenty-eight miles west of Land's End. Alan Nance was born at St. Mary's, the largest island of the archipelago, in 1898.

" You must see a big difference in the Scillies now, a very different place from the islands you knew as a boy."

A broad grin swept across his face :

" You can say that it stinks now. St. Mary's is almost completely changed, its character and its inhabitants. St. Agnes of the inhabited islands is about the only unspoilt one."

A painting from the island, hung on the wall. Daymark on St. Martin's, two indentations : Bread and Cheese Cove and Stony Par, a morning setting.

"My parents were Methodists and I went through the usual Methodist ritual of those times : Chapel, Sunday School, Harvest Festival, Band of Hope, the lot . . . not that it made very much impact. I don't think I even thought about religion seriously. Looking back now, I realise the preachers and Sunday School teachers were offering something very abstract."

At the age of fourteen, he went to sea, a voyage which stretched eastward as far as Burma, Rangoon and the Black Sea. In 1916 he joined The Duke of Cornwall's Light Infantry, served in France, and was blown up on the way to Passchendale.

"German artillery, a terrific shock it was . . . my last conscious memory of the explosion was the sight of a mate, blood pouring out of his mouth . . . but I recovered." Exchanging a soldier's uniform for civilian clothes, Alan Nance came westward again. Between the wars he lived initially at Plymouth, where he learnt watchmaking, and later on the Scillies. Then in 1950 wanderlust stirred and he emigrated to Australia.

"A brother of mine had been out there since the twenties, and I thought I'd like to go out and see him." Combining watch repairs and electrical work, he lived in a caravan and roamed all over Australia for seven years.

Australia, in fact, produced important cross-roads in his life. There he met Bill Austen, an ex-editor of *Psychic News*, and his wife. "Paulette was a wonderful medium and through their experiences I became really interested in the subject of spiritualism."

"When did you begin healing ?"

"It must have been around 1956. I didn't start healing right away. I'd once come across a book by Hannen Swaffer, in which he'd warned people not to meddle in spiritualism without help and guidance. Actually I started on myself, with myself as the patient. I was having considerable trouble with my left eye. It ached and ached ; so, one night, I asked for healing. Next morning, the eye was as right as rain. I was absolutely shattered but, on reflection, I saw it as practical proof of healing power."

Before returning to England, Alan Nance received news that his sister had a cyst in her breast.

"I just asked for healing again, as I'd done with my eye trouble and, when I arrived back in England, I learned the cyst had gone. There was proof again . . ."

Back in Cornwall, this time St. Austell, Alan Nance began to think seriously about his potential as a healer.

" I was staying as a paying guest in a house nearby, and one of the women there, had to go into hospital. Once more I asked for healing. When she got into hospital, they could find nothing wrong with her !"

" What brought you to St. Austell ?"

" Something seemed to direct me here. Maybe it had something to do with the fact that I used to come here to do some shooting in the 1930's and 1940's. I also thought, rather than working for somebody else, I'd like to go into business on my own, and St. Austell seemed a pretty good place to start. I couldn't find any vacant premises down in the town, but, one day, walking over the railway bridge, I saw this empty shop in Trevarthian Road . . . I made enquiries and have been here ever since, except for a spell of eighteen months, when I went to London to study healers at work.

" In the beginning, it was a question of finding victims ! There was a friend of mine, living just outside St. Austell, she had a gastric ulcer. I asked her if I could try spiritual healing. 'Not likely !' She and her husband and I had quite an argument about it. Anyway, just to shut me up, they let me have a go. I didn't have to ask her a second time. The next time I called, she was delighted to see me for another healing. Within two months, the ulcer had healed completely."

Alan Nance is a deceptive figure. You would never think of him as a man into his seventies. There is a merry twinkle in the eye ; his swift, certain movements suggest a man appreciably younger. In his grey suit with white shirt and red tie, he might be taken for a civil servant or a schoolmaster or a bank clerk. Only his sandals tell you he is not - that and his total disinterest in money. He refuses to take a penny from his patients. He talks quietly, words flow naturally ; a remarkable vocabulary for a man whose formal education ended at the age of thirteen. He has blue, penetrating eyes ; his handshake is strong.

I have watched him healing : a simple laying-on of hands, usually on the spine, sometimes on the affected area, never any ritual.

" Healing is uplifting for me " he said, " I experience a certain glow after treating a case. If I've had a really busy day with healings, I feel absolutely fine . . . have had between twenty and thirty this week. The nature of God, nobody knows . . . but I visualise an immense reservoir of love and power. I'm merely the channel of that love and power. I'm the last link in the chain ;

down from the ultimate to me and into the patient. If a patient were to receive direct from God or The Great White Spirit - call it what you will - he'd be shrivelled, the power has to be diluted. It's a delegation of power. If you want a simple, worldly illustration : think of the captain on board ship. He doesn't go dashing all over the ship, he delegates responsibility. This life force in healing comes through a long chain of command. I believe that healing is a means of the spirits proving that there is survival after death.

"My spirit guide is a North American Indian. He lived on earth about seven-hundred years ago . . . no, I can't give you his name, but I will tell you he's a member of the Pawnee tribe. No, I've never seen him. Other people have described him to me. Mediums have seen him. But I get messages from him clearly, easily. Just before going to sleep for the night or first thing in the mornings are the best times, you're more relaxed then, more receptive."

" In spiritual healing, does diagnosis help ?"

"It may help, certainly helps the patient to be able to talk about his or her particular trouble ; but the healers in spirit are able to do their own diagnosis."

" What goes through your mind when you've your hand on a patient ?"

Another broad smile.

"All sorts of thoughts. I must confess! To begin with, I concentrate very hard, but after a time, my mind often strays on to all sorts of subjects. It doesn't seem to make any difference though, the healing power still travels through to the patient. In a very serious case, I concentrate all the time, like the one I visited this afternoon." Alan Nance had been to a Cornish hospital, where a young woman was lying unconscious : the result of a motoring accident on the A.30, in which her sister had been killed a week before. " She opened her eyes for the first time yesterday. There was a glimmer of recognition. For a few seconds her eyes followed her mother." *

Anyone, outside the fold of Spiritualist philosophy, is likely to find conversation with Alan Nance slightly disconcerting, for he talks of spirit people as most individuals talk of their friends, their neighbours, their business associates. The departed are not merely memories. They are - to him and many other Spiritualists - intensely alive, and through a medium, capable of communication. Some months ago he was distressed over the death of a young patient. But he claims she, via a medium's message, told him not to be sad; she had been helped "on the other side" by an old friend of the healer's. "I know she's in good hands . . . and now I communicate with her myself."

°A fortnight after our interview at St. Austell. Alan Nance wrote to me. "I have been going to Jenny at Treliske - the car accident casualty - nearly every day and there is gradual improvement. Her mother and husband have been unable to get there for the last three days by reason of the snow, but I have been. Today they phoned and arranged to link up with me at the time I should be giving her healing, about 5.45 p.m. I reached the hospital at 5.25 and sat in a chair on the landing to get attunement with them which commenced almost at once. At 5.35 I went to her ward and told the Sister what we were doing - spiritual healing is fully accepted. At 5.40 I laid hands on her, and could feel the power building up, I have only experienced it once before, when a woman with three weeks to live was cleared of all cancer in ten days and downstairs walking around in a month. Within five minutes my breathing was being controlled, my head was swimming, and I was semi-tranced, the power making my whole body feel afire, it was also having its effect on Jenny, her body, arms and legs were moving, her eyes opening and closing, and her mouth, and she gave several deep breaths, which I had not seen her do before. After I had finished giving her healing, the Sister wanted me to sit down for a few minutes. I must have looked (I felt) squiffy, but I knew I should be looked after, so walked back to the station to catch the 6.27. Her mother and husband are also healers, which is why they could reach me with such force, but it was revelation to me taking everything into consideration, I never cease to wonder at the marvel of it all, there are no words to express it."

I asked about death.

"Death's only a door opening. I have no fear. When the time comes for me to go, I shall go without a tinge of regret. Death really comes as a friend. This material world is the fantasy. The other is reality."

I asked him about failures, patients who die.

"Some cases don't apparently respond. There was the case of Harry Edwards attempting to cure Jack Webber. Webber died. Why ? We don't know. What is failure ? Without healing, some people might have suffered more. I knew a cancer case; the young man never experienced pain after healing had commenced. Was that failure ? Healing shuts off areas of pain."

"Is there a sense of conflict between you and medical science ? Is there a time when you say to yourself: 'This person should go to a doctor ?'"

"Not conflict. There are times when I do recommend a patient to go to their doctor. I only wish it worked the other way, and that doctors would send some of their patients to me. There's where he conflict lies. The majority of doctors are still very hostile on the subject of spiritual healing. Tolerance is coming but very slowly. In London, for example, more and more hospitals now willingly open their doors to spiritual healers. Did you know in Brazil doctors and spiritual healers have been working together for thirty years? That's what we want to see in this country."

Following our conversation in the flat, I visited one of Alan Nance's patients.

A male nurse, with twenty years experience behind him, I pictured him, in my mind's eye, five years ago: the type of character you would have found in the engine room of a rugby scrum. He had done in his time - and still does - some impressive weightlifting. He was thirty-eight. Two years before, he had contracted lymphosarcoma, a most rapid form of cancer. He went to London, was examined by one of the greatest authorities on the disease, and became a patient at a famous London hospital. But treatment induced no improvement. His wife, a former nurse, told me how she had been given a virtual death sentence: 'Your husband may last another two years. Take him back to Cornwall, and make life as pleasant as possible for him.' They have two children. He came back to Cornwall a doomed man. A friend suggested he should see Alan Nance. Initially the idea was rejected, but eventually he reluctantly agreed and went along to Trevarthian Road.

"Originally I had three lumps, one on my neck, one under my arm and one in my groin." He sat on the chair opposite me, a cup of tea in his hand, his spectacles stuck in his hair: an unconsciously comical pose. But it wasn't funny. I had done some hasty arithmetic and calculated this man should be dead in a matter of weeks. "Alan's healing is working. The lump on my neck and in my groin have gone, and the one under my arm has grown smaller. My blood count is almost normal. The last time I went to London for a check-up, I think they expected me to crawl in! I'd say they're a bit perplexed. With all my medical training, I can't logically say I'm cured but I *feel* cured . . ." Alan Nance looked across at him: "Your medical training is your biggest handicap." He said it with a smile.

Later in the evening, at Holmbush, on the outskirts of St. Austell, I met Danny Warren, then a fifteen year old pupil of the Penrice School.

Danny was born with a hole in his heart. "An operation was out of the question" his mother explained "it was too risky. Better to have a son fifty per cent alive than one-hundred per cent dead, that's what the doctor said." "When I used to take him to play ball on the green," said Mr. Warren, "Danny used to come in after five minutes, finished. He'd just stretch out, his face like a brandy bottle, at times he'd go purple." Alan Nance appeared on the scene when Danny was nine. In two months a transformation. Today Danny plays soccer and cricket, rides a cycle and swims.

"Quite a change Danny?"

"Oh, yes, it's a different life altogether. I can remember the heat when Mr. Nance laid his hands on me. Like two hot water bottles, that might be an apt description."

"Did you think Mr. Nance could do what medical people had failed to achieve?"

Danny's father, in an open neck shirt, was sitting on the other side of the table; cards were sprawled over the cloth. Father and son had been in the middle of a game of Lexicon.

"You asked me a straight question, mister, and I'll give you a straight answer. No, I didn't think he could cure the boy, I'll put it this way, I hoped but I didn't have confidence . . . but a drowning man will see a plank, will clutch anything, won't he?"

Danny however, was not the only shadow falling across the Warren family at that time. His sister, Annette, five years his senior, was also critically ill. Alan Nance recalled Annette's difficulties: "At fourteen she had experienced a stiffness in her left arm which was attributed to over-exercise at games. When a lump was found under her arm, she went to her doctor, who at once sent her to Truro, where a section of it was taken for biopsy. Although recognised as cancer, specimens were sent to several places, including America. One specialist gave her little more than six months." Spiritual healing went on for three months, after which Annette was sent to Bristol for cobalt bomb treatment; she was away about seven weeks. She returned to Cornwall, in her own words, "in a shattered condition, very on edge, very nervous." Her mother was told the treatment had made her sterile. In the event of her marrying, she wouldn't be able to bear any children. On her return to Cornwall, spiritual healing was resumed; a later check-up by the doctors revealed no traces of cancer. "I don't claim to have solely cured Annette," reflected Alan Nance as he sat beside the Warrens' fire, "it could be called a co-operative effort with the medical profession."

"A wonderful peace came over me, whenever Mr. Nance put his hands on my spine" was Annette's recollection. She was sitting on the sofa, alongside her husband, holding her baby, feeding him from a bottle: the same blue eyes as his mother and grandmother. His little brother has blue eyes too.

Mrs. Warren looked at her grandchildren, then switched her gaze to me : "Those two children of Annette's are a miracle."

Alan Nance, allowing himself the slightest of smiles, kept looking into the fire.

ROSEANNON 9

Curing a Dog

My meetings with Charlie Bennett and Alan Nance roughly coincided with reading a book by Angela du Maurier.

One of Gerald du Maurier's three daughters, she lives at Ferryside, Bodinnick-by-Fowey on the sheltered southern side of Cornwall. The book was *Old Maids Remember* in which she reminisced, cleverly arranging her recollections in alphabetical order : A for age, B for beauty, C for children and childhood. It was D for dogs which held my interest most.

Angela du Maurier explained how her dog Tony, at the age of one, had lost all his fur. " This could have been the result of several things, shock from a severe operation for one of the worst hernias the Vet said he had ever known, or it could have been the result of hormone injections for something else. No matter, he was as bare as a tiny elephant. I thought him rather enchanting, but there were people who wondered why I did not 'put him down.' Friends of mine valiantly strove with hair-restorer, and in time he grew a superlative coat which caused admiration wherever he went. But - and this is a very strange story : at a hairdresser's one day I read in a magazine a strange article about an animal sanctuary, where 'absent' healing had done miraculous cures. I sent up Tony's name and details of the illness he had suffered, and a little while later hair began to sprout. When Cleo (another of the author's dogs) had two desperate illnesses, poisoning from slug death and another time meningitis, with all the devoted care from the Vet (whom she loves dearly) I definitely believe that prayers from the animal sanctuary helped in a miraculous way. And I have one more story apropos : years ago I won money on a beautiful horse, Tulyar (Derby winner, etc.) He was sold to the United States and soon after arrival developed some strange illness which, according to the English press, put paid to his future career. He was a noble animal, and I could not bear to think of such an un-fitting end, so I sent his name to the sanctuary. I forget how long afterwards it was, more than a year, maybe two, I read in a Sunday newspaper 'Miraculous Recovery of Race Horse': it was Tulyar. I felt I had in some little way helped. It was a wonderful thing to read."

Angela du Maurier's Tony cured, Cleo helped, and a Derby winner all restored by absent healing? "Why not Tex, our terrier?" I asked.

Tex was usually a bundle of tan and white, long-haired energy, but the previous summer, a shadow had fallen. Tex had developed 'a leg.' For the past two years he had been suffering from a kneecap periodically slipping out. The Veterinary Surgeon, an affable fellow Cornishman in practice at Camelford, assured us the kneecap - he used its correct, technical title - would slip back of its own accord. And he was absolutely right. Sometimes, in only a matter of an hour or two, the kneecap went back into place, and Tex became his old energetic self again. Against this background of Nature's own cure, nobody at Bossiney House was perturbed. Tex would be alright tomorrow or the next day, in the meantime he was given a painkilling tablet, concealed in some meat, but this time Tax was not right, either tomorrow or the following day. For once Nature's way was not working, and a whole week later Tex was still unhappy.

Our Veterinary Surgeon is a brave man, he deserved a medal every time he examined his punacious little patient. Time was when Tex had been ill treated and he had not forgotten those days. The legacy of that unhappy period was a distrust of people. Tex was prepared to make friends but only on his terms, and his terms did not include being stroked or picked up. Three people were allowed these intimacies, and only they took the liberty, when the mood was right. Unfortunately, Tex's MO was not one of the favoured trio. However, amid much growling, then squealing and display of teeth, an examination was made: it was not the old trouble. A more thorough examination under anaesthetic followed at the Camelford surgery; Tex's doctor plus his partner went over every inch of the affected area and arthritis was the verdict. A month's course of steroid tablets and tonic were prescribed.

August slipped away, summer turned to autumn and Tex still carried that rear leg at the trot. Occasionally when he landed heavily or awkwardly, in descent from chair to floor, he would cry out. He was in less discomfort generally; he was eating well, and he was capable of walking normally. The sight of a bouncing ball or the sudden appearance of a cat were still means of sending him into top gear. Moreover the Veterinary Surgeon assured us there was no need for mournful thoughts about his being put down.

Sadly, grudgingly I began to accept a fact: Tex was much better - thanks to Veterinary skill - but he would never be one hundred per cent fit again.

Reading Angela du Maurier's book however, revised my thinking on the subject. "Why not Tex indeed?" I resolved to get in touch with the Sanctuary and wrote to Miss du Maurier, asking for the address. Her reply was a bitter blow: the Santuary was no longer in existence. Soon after this disappointment, a neighbour at Bossiney told me how, some years ago, her dog had been successfully treated through spiritual healing. This news only steeled my determination to find a healer for Tex.

Was there perhaps one in Cornwall who specialized in healing animals?

I was determined to find out.

• • •

We talked in one of the cottage's two downstairs rooms.

Outside, it was a December morning borrowed from midsummer with blue skies and scarcely a cloud. Brilliant sunlight was giving everything a golden, almost theatrical glow. Birds were singing in a nearby cluster of trees. A black cat was staring at us through an open door.

"Healing's a kind of secret," she said. Knowledge that I was a writer had suddenly set her defensive mechanism into motion. Enquiring brown eyes moved from me to Tex who was on his lead alongside. "If I cure your little dog, you can mention that in your book, but I don't want my name mentioned. As I say, healing's a kind of secret. What's wrong with the little dog?"

She was choosing words slowly, almost nervously.

Photographs of friends and relations surrounded us, many of them yellow and curled with age. She settled herself on the chair opposite: an elderly woman with a pinafore and sallow complexion; hair hidden beneath black netting.

A farmer's wife had told me about this healer. She had cured a stallion of ringworm around an eye within the space of seven days. Moreover her powers were not confined to animals. I was told of a woman suffering from asthma, who had come here and had received considerable benefit. And, from another source, I heard of a young farming student suffering from sores on the arm. The healer sent him a handkerchief, instructed him to wear it around the affected area for three days, and then to burn it. Instructions obeyed, the sores disappeared on the fourth day.

I explained the Veterinary Surgeon's diagnosis : arthritis in the hip. She listened intently.

" Have you got a little coat, he can wear ?"

I told her Tex had never worn one in his life, implying we might lose a finger if we tried to persuade him.

The fact that he was an aggressive animal, capable of drawing blood, seemed of no concern. " We could wrap bandages around his sore part." Again I expressed doubt. She looked thoughtful, said nothing. I wondered whether she would show me the door.

" Have you a rug he sleeps on ?" she asked, " that would do."

It was back in Tintagel, but I offered to call back in the afternoon ; in the meantime I'd get some material at Wadebridge.

" Yes " she said " that'll be alright. I shall be here . . . shall be here until midnight. You never know who's going to walk through the door." She went back to her stew in the kitchen ; Tex and I clambered back into the car. As we were pulling away, another car halted outside the cottage. A man, carrying a blanket, knocked at the door.

It was almost two o'clock, when I got back to the cottage. I had had a drink and a sandwich at The Molesworth Arms, after buying one and a half yards of Winceyette at Treleavens. " We've only white or pale blue " the girl behind the counter had said. I had chosen the latter. I had remembered some advice too. " She won't take any money." So I had bought some food as a gift.

Shadows were lengthening and a chill was creeping into the day as we travelled back.

" The lady what's just gone. She's wonderfully brave. She believes I can cure her. She drove all the way up from the Land's End." The reticence of the morning had receded. " I've done some marvellous things with dogs. Had one a month ago, he was dropped there on that mat, and didn't move ; the Vets said he would have to be put down. The man and woman didn't have any children, the dog sort of took the place of children; they brought the dog back last week. He jumped over the wall. She didn't smile, merely spread the material in her lap, the rest stretched across the table. Boney hands moved swiftly over the material ; at times, she plunged fingers and thumbs into the pale blue, then she switched to a gentle form of stroking, rather like somebody flicking away invisible crumbs. " Tex, nice doggie !" She smiled for the first time. Tex looked back knowingly, his head on one side, his ears pricked. " We'll get you better."

“ What mystifies me ” I said, “ is how you do it with animals. If a man or a woman comes to you, they've faith in you. But a dog hasn't faith - has he ?”

She looked at me sharply.

“ But you, sir, you've faith . . . ” Her boney hand pointed, first at me, then at Tex. “ Your faith, that'll go through to the little dog. He'll get it.” Tex's head remained slanted ; his eyes never leaving her. All the while her hands continued to work across the material.

“ Does it make you tired ?”

“ Oh, yes. If I have to do a lot of garments, I feel very tired at the end of the day. I do pants and vests for people, wrap them up in a parcel and send them off. I've got a vest to go to Crantock by this afternoon's post . . it must go, the man's very ill.

“ This healing takes a lot out of you . . . I shan't be sorry if there are no more visitors today. But there'll be some parcels when the postman calls this afternoon. There nearly always are . . .

“ When you get home, I want you to cut this material into four equal pieces ; use each piece for a week as the top part of the little dog's bed each night ” she said, picking up a black biro. I watched her make a cross in each corner of the Winceyette. “ I've made the cross, so that the cloth is that way up ” she explained, “ I want his body, at night, resting against that side of the material.

Back in Tintagel, early that evening, as an experiment, I put a segment of the cloth on a cushion in one of the armchairs in the lounge, and Tex settled himself. Normally he was a restless spirit ; half an hour in one chair, then down on the rug before the log fire. Later perhaps over to the sofa or if he wanted a lower temperature, across the room to a cooler spot by the window. On this particular evening, once settled on the Winceyette, all desire to roam died and he remained asleep on the same chair for the greater part of five hours. Coincidence ? Perhaps, but I am only relating the facts. At night too Tex's behaviour underwent a distinct change. Most nights for the next month, he was content to sleep peacefully on the material until next morning.

Two months passed and Tex was now sleeping without the Winceyette. Had he been cured ? I found it a difficult question, for though he still moved largely on three legs, the suspect rear leg was used in what I called the walk and the gallop, but never in the trot. “ It's a mental rut,” somebody said, “ he's got into the habit of carrying it. He'll never use it properly again.”

Then suddenly one day I noticed him moving at the trot on all four legs. From that day he never again moved on three legs.

SALTASH 10

UFOs & Healing

On Saturday evening, 23rd October 1971, parts of Cornwall had a television blackout with viewers finding their pictures fading or others superimposed.

A BBC spokesman referred to "circumstances beyond our control," and a Westward official for Independent television blamed "propagation trouble," explaining that this was the propagation of radio waves in the atmosphere which affected the actual microwavelengths used in television transmission. South-western radio also suffered in that there was extensive Continental interference.

More than thirty people telephoned television and radio stations and newspaper offices reporting a strange sight in the sky.

Two years and four months later, one grey, cold February morning, I travelled south-east to Saltash to meet one of those eye-witnesses. Standing on the bank of the River Tamar, Saltash is literally a gateway to Cornwall. Viewed from the eastward English bank, from the Plymouth side, Saltash looks like a mediaeval town with its houses, grey and white, rising one above another on the sharply angled hillside.

Mrs. Marilyn Preston greeted me at the door of her home with two dogs and a tame pigeon fluttering above them in the hallway. A Devonian by birth: "I was born on Plymouth Hoe in 1933 . . . no, not on one of the benches! My parents ran a fruit and grocery business on the Hoe at Windsor Lane." She now lives in a solid-looking terrace house not far from Brunel's famous bridge which still carries trains over the Tamar.

Sitting in a comfortable armchair with a ginger cat purring contentedly in her lap, she remembered that unusual October evening quite clearly. "I was travelling back from Launceston with a Vegan friend Michael Mansergh when about 6.15 at Ellbridge, near Saltash, we were suddenly attracted by a strange, large pink and golden ball of light in the sky. In an attempt to

Waterfall at St. Nectan's Glen:
"Full of poetry and coloured by legend . . . a *feeling* that *something* happened here." Chapter 5

Methodist Chapel at Bossiney : " . . . a light suddenly appeared . . . it grew - a glow rather than a single shaft of electricity . . ." Chapter 6

Bossiney Mound: "Legend has it that King Arthur's round table lies buried beneath . . . and that it comes to the surface one night a year . . ." Chapter 6

On the summit of Rough Tor:
" Tex was not to be enticed. He refused to go another inch, instead he shook like a seriously-ill animal." Chapter 6

get a closer look at this mysterious object, Michael drove west on the Pillaton Road but the light disappeared. Disappointed we returned to the precise spot where we had made the original sighting. We waited for a few minutes watching a perfectly clear sky. There was no question of cloud effects or the moon or the sun playing tricks. It was an empty sky. Then suddenly the UFO reappeared in the same spot where we had seen it before, but this time in the shape of a cigar, although the colour remained the same. Whilst we watched, it changed shape six times in about 30 minutes, in accord with our conversations as to what experts might say it was. Slowly, we realized the space ship was attuned to our thought-waves, and when it finally went we contacted the press and television studios."

Marilyn Preston firmly believes this was an object from another planet. Moreover she bases her belief on the strength of an earlier experience, "an astral projection," she called it which happened on 6th September 1971.

"I pinched myself to make sure I was not simply asleep and dreaming. Physically I was in bed upstairs here, but I do assure you that I was on Plymouth Hoe in an equally real sense, or rather more so, and there I met and spoke with a tall spaceman who told me that he and his colleagues came to help us. He radiated tremendous love and compassion, not of an Earthly capacity, and said 'We came in Love and Peace to help you . . . will you not accept us in Love and Peace?' He received my thoughts and added 'Yes, we are speaking telepathically as we always used to do.' His large silver craft bore white, yellow, blue and green lights. Previous to this happening I had never thought much about UFOs or Flying Saucers and was not aware of the hundreds of books and articles on the subject and the dozens of Light Centres connected with Space People and their crafts.

"The next morning I was terribly excited and wanted to tell everybody, but was uncertain whether I should tell anyone. 'They'll think I'm mad!' I thought. Then that evening on television the announcer said that a UFO had been sighted near the Saltash area . . . I immediately wrote to television and radio studios about the experience I had had the night before, giving them the full content of the Space Being's message. Next day a press item gave the news that people from Callington, not far from here, had witnessed the UFO and with precisely the same coloured lights I had seen in astral travel which verified that part of my experience. Six months later I contacted my first Light Centre in Solihull and was surprised to find that the founder had been given an identical telepathic message during November to the one I had received on the 6th September."

At a meeting of the Plymouth Astronomical Society in November, 1972 Marilyn Preston talked frankly about her UFO experiences and found a ready ally in Society member Stephen Johnson. He argued that such unexplained sightings should be given more credence, publicity and investigating time and that such sightings did probably involve visits to this planet by more advanced civilizations existing elsewhere in the universe. Dr. James McDonald, Senior Physicist, Institute of Atmospheric Physics, University of Arizona, speaking on the subject of extraterrestrial vehicles, said "There are certain patterns that suggest that the UFOs are engaged in something of the nature of reconnaissance. I regard this as the number one problem before science."

Marilyn Preston's whole life style changed in 1969: "I was feeling very depressed, sorry for myself, down with a sore throat and could hardly speak. Then out of the blue, through the post, I received a bottle of Flower Power from someone who had read something I'd written in the press denouncing the tortures of animal experimentation. I thought I couldn't very well write back saying 'I've thrown it away!' so took it, expecting that I could politely reply 'Thank you very much for sending the flower medicine - I've tried it but it didn't work.' However, the following day I felt much better and more uplifted and by the end of the week I felt a new person and really positive for the first time in my whole life. All this coincided with my reading a book by Air Chief Marshal Lord Dowding *Lychgate - The Entrance to the Path* which introduced me to Spiritualism and a completely new way of living and thinking."

Spiritualism, at the same time, led her to spiritual healing. She dislikes the term faith healing "because many patients come to healers having lost their faith completely in just about everything and everyone. Spiritual healing, as I see it at the moment, isn't depending on the patient believing or disbelieving. Quite a few sceptics come here, literally dragged by a friend or a relation, and the power has still worked. Some come with all the faith in the world and no cure is forthcoming. Actually I started with animals and birds, having treated and cared for many hundreds of them for about 10 years previously, but only by orthodox methods."

Her concern for the animal kingdom is such that she has become a Vegan. "That means I eat nothing at all that comes from the animal world, nor do I use or wear such items. I'm nearly a fruit and nut case! Seriously though I am, in fact, hoping to become a fruitarian . . . I'm convinced that by a Vegan diet you can and do achieve a greater spiritual quality.

"I can still clearly remember the Saturday in 1969 when a voice distinctly said to me in our kitchen: 'Lyn you're a hypocrite! You call yourself an animal lover and yet you eat the corpses of animals and birds.' The voice said that if I was to complete the mission I came to the Earth plane to do, I was not to exploit the animal kingdom in any way at all, in order to attune to the powers surrounding us on higher frequencies. The voice again spoke to me when I was about to have kippers for tea that evening; and on the following day it coldly asked 'How many more times? You have the free will to choose which path to travel, but remember what I told you yesterday!' Then there was silence and I was left wondering. Like the ham in the salad the previous day and the five little kipper fillets, the chicken remained on my plate and I've never had flesh foods or animal products since . . . that was five years ago and in those five years I've only been to the doctor once for a diagnosis whereas previously I was in and out of doctors' surgeries and hospitals all my life. Now I'm a much more positive person. I used to be terrified of people before! But my new state of being isn't just by being a Vegan alone. It's rather a combination of Veganism, free-thinking, being a loner and a rebel and accepting, in the main, Spiritualist principles and teachings."

Compassion for all dumb creatures has turned Marilyn Preston into a militant anti-vivisectionist. With anger hardening her voice she explained "I see the vivisector today in the role of the priest of Black Magic, wrestling his secrets at the expense of great suffering. All life is one - thats' my philosophy. You see it is important for people to realize that what they are inflicting in the way of pain and suffering on any other form of life *has* to boomerang to humanity. We are involved here with the Law of Karma - better known as Cause and Effect. Whatever we cause, has to have an effect to the same or more intensified degree. That's the Law and we cannot change it."

A loyal supporter of Beauty Without Cruelty, she prefers her soaps, shampoos, cosmetics etc. to come from flowers, herbs and plants, sources that involve no animal suffering. Over coffee and in front of an electric fire, set in a hand-cut Cornish granite fire-place made by her husband, I brought our conversation back to spiritual healing.

"Can you remember your first patient?"

Marilyn Preston smiled broadly and stroked the ginger cat who had settled once more in her lap. "Yes, he was a pet rabbit somebody did not want and had left here. A Dutch one, he was going blind. 'I'll try healing it myself,' I said, and the next day the eye was clear and the scar gone. 'It works!' Tremendous excitement . . . and I went on from there. Gaining confidence through birds and animals I progressed to human beings. But it greatly concerns me that the majority of patients are terrified of informing their doctors and surgeons that they have been cured or helped by spiritual healing. One patient was immediately discharged from hospital when the Consultant found she had been treated by a healer there. Yet other Surgeons have been extremely kind and helpful in allowing me to treat patients . . . one Surgeon brought his wife here for treatment and insisted I treat him at the same time.

" A friend, a dear old soul, was thrown out of the Roman Catholic Church because she communicates with her 'dead' family. Through her, a voice told me my first patient would be a crippled man on the doorstep. Six months later I answered the front door to find my first human patient - a young man crippled in a road accident a year before, still on crutches after five operations. Six months later he was walking very well, his open flesh wound from the accident having healed in about two weeks following healing and the leg bone then knitting together easily - healing was achieved through a full leg plaster. Like all healers I feel elated with success - not because it is a personal thing for me, but because the patient has been at a stage when he or she has been able to respond to the healing and receive it. Often they are changed people. But don't forget it's not me . . . I'm merely the channel of the healing power and thousands of people can be used for healing and other spiritual purposes, if they apply themselves and develop their latent potential abilities. Following healing one's batteries can become almost flat, but this doesn't often happen."

Tropical fish darted in a tank in the corner of the room.

" And what about failures ?"

She looked rather sad. " That's difficult. It could be for any number of reasons, including Karma. But even if one fails to effect a complete cure, one at least aims to give the patient a peace of mind, easement and possibly removal of tensions, so that they can more readily accept their condition in a happier frame of mind . . . and that's quite something. Some are able to be helped through into the next stage of life ; some have literally given up the ghost, have lost the will to live, and others have definitely had a call from the Other Side. If it's time to leave this plane of life, they return home to spirit, but no-one dies, not even our little friends, the birds and animals, which has been proved, of course, by many Spiritualists and others. I have spoken with spirit doctors - they often have a remarkable sense of humour on the Other Side of life."

"How do you define spiritual healing?"

The sadness suddenly went from her face. " I think I would call it spiritual power, energy or electricity. It's interesting that sometimes when I've been healing we've had happenings with electrical appliances, and I'm not talking about power cuts and things like that but instances of where fires, lights and other apparatus have behaved abnormally. Only recently I was called to heal a man unable to walk with spinal and ankle damages as shown by X-ray ; that morning he had been transported to and from hospital by stretcher for further X-rays. During healing his tropical fish tank lights went off and on four times and at the end of the hour he found he was completely cured, though during the actual hour of treatment he had been unconscious."

Vicky, the ginger cat, stirred and stretched. " She was a pretty hopeless case," Marilyn Preston explained, "the Veterinary Surgeon said it was best to put her out of her misery. She had a broken thigh and other fractures in her hind leg, having been run over by a car. For ten days she lay in a basket in our bathroom and I fed her by hand and gave spiritual healing. There was progress right away. Soon she was purring and showing no sign of pain. By this time I found I could apply mental plasters to patients, human and animal, and this has been *felt* being applied by humans . . . it keeps the physical bone in place until healing is completed . . . but unfortunately it doesn't always work. Anyway mentally I put a plaster on Vicky's leg and on the 11th day she began to walk around."

One of Marilyn Preston's dogs is another ex-patient. " Again it was suggested that he should be put down, in fact he was brought here just two hours before he was due to have a final injection. He had brain and spinal damage following a car accident and he was suffering from hardpad. But as you saw just now he's full of bounce . . . too much bounce at times !"

There are 30 birds at present occupying open aviaries in the small garden at the back of the house. " I attribute my interest in birds to the war years when I was evacuated down to my grandparents in Mousehole and saw the wonderful work being done there at the bird hospital by the Yglesias sisters."

Anyone, doubting Marilyn Preston's gift of helping others, should see the written testimonials, shoals of them from former patients. Time and again, reading through them, one is aware of tensions and anxieties removed. Apart from a laying-on of hands and absent healing, Marilyn Preston is also an advocate of Dr. Edward Bach's Flower Remedies from plants, trees and herbs. " These can remove disease and take away fears and worries, leaving us happier in ourselves by healing our personalities."

"How do you see your future as a healer developing?" I asked. The hands of the clock were past noon and I knew there would be a long line of patients during the afternoon and evening.

A thoughtful look came back into her face. "I'd like to have a lovely sanctuary for animals and birds and people in desperate need of healing, without having to live on a shoestring, somewhere peaceful in the country. But a spirit doctor has said that my work is to be on another dimension entirely. Perhaps it will be with our Space Friends. We shall have to wait and see."

LOSTWITHIEL 11

The Squire

Now my supernatural search moved south-east.

More than once in the process of these journeys, across the county, I had been struck by the fact that certain regions, within the context of supernatural claims, have been barren. Callington and Liskeard, for example, Torpoint, Looe and Polperro all failed to produce a single claim. Lostwithiel however did produce something.

Lostwithiel, at the head of the long Fowey estuary, is twenty-eight miles from Launceston. In the 13th century it was the Cornish capital and Cornwall's only stannary town; miners brought their metal here to have it stamped, assayed and taxed. Part of the old stannary building remains, heavily buttressed and now a Masonic Hall. It was at Lostwithiel, by the font of the parish church, that Roundheads christened a horse 'Charlie,' in mockery of the King.

Roughly a mile away, high above the town, is the house of Pelyn. Once the heart of a two-thousand acre estate and home to generations of Kendalls. (The family came to Cornwall around 1200). Drives converge from right and left - on the left, the drive cuts through pleasant parkland punctuated by trees and grazing cattle ; from the right, the avenue is flanked by lofty trees of beech, oak and fir. A manor house has been here since the Norman Conquest.

Present owners and occupants of Pelyn are Nicholas Kendall, a former High Sheriff of Cornwall, and his wife Frances.

"We've heard it said the Kendalls had more Cornish MP's than any other family" they told me. Born at Chichester in 1903, Nicholas Kendall has lived at Pelyn since 1918. Educated at Harrow, he served for a while in the Coldstream Guards, married his wife - also Cornish - in 1925, and has been looking after Pelyn ever since. His chief interests are the RSPCA and Cornwall's Historic Churches Trust, of which he is Chairman.

It was Frances Kendall who gave me the following account :

" In the early part of this century there lived a blacksmith at Castle Dore, near Fowey. He was a teetotaller, a good hard-working man. Once a week he used to walk to Lostwithiel, a distance of some four to five miles, to see friends. On one occasion when he had crossed from the Fowey road to the main one running down to Lostwithiel, he noticed another man ahead of him, walking in the same direction. The man was tall, upright, but walked with a stick in his hand, and was striding along at a good pace. The blacksmith couldn't see his face but his attention was caught by the rather old-fashioned clothes which the man wore. The blacksmith quickened his pace so that he could get a closer clearer look. Just before he reached Pelyn drive gate however, he tripped on a stone in the road and, to his astonishment, when he looked up the other man had completely disappeared.

The blacksmith continued on his way to Lostwithiel and reported the strange experience to his friends in the town. Knowing he was a teetotaller, they started to pull his leg : 'You must water 'en down, Ernie, before you tell that there tale ; for what you'ne tellin' you seen, was old Squire Kendall, and 'e been dead now'n twenty years !' The old blacksmith, though, stuck to his story, and it's survived to this day. I was told all this by a member of the Fowey Old Cornwall Society who knew the old blacksmith."

The old squire, was, in fact, another Nicholas Kendall. He came with the century, born in 1800 and succeeded his father at the age of twenty-six. Three years before he had married Mary Ann Wymond - they had four children - three sons and a daughter who eventually married Sir Colman Rashleigh. Squire Kendall was a great character. He had many friends, and a few enemies too - mostly political. He was Conservative MP for East Cornwall from 1852 until 1868, when Gladstone's first Liberal ministry began, and was involved in many political storms. An ancient newspaper cutting tells how he rode off one day, to quell some rioting near Bodmin, where he arrested sixteen men singlehanded and promptly marched them to the county gaol. At the age of seventy, he found himself out of Parliament, but took a new lease of life by accepting the office of Chief Magistrate of Gibraltar. Discovering a knowledge of Spanish would be helpful, he proceeded to learn the language ! He finally retired to Pelyn and died there in '78, two years after Bell's invention of the telephone.

The squire's portrait hangs at Pelyn today, above a marble chimney piece in the ballroom, the work of an unknown artist. " I don't suppose it's a very valuable painting," Nicholas Kendall admitted as we stood before it, "but we're extremely glad to have it. It was originally in an Institution in Bodmin but when the place was closed down, it was passed on to Pelyn. Date? Probably somewhere in the 1850's, that wouldn't be far out."

The present master of Pelyn has had the peculiar sensation of seeing the estate gates open and close on a walk up the drive. "They opened just as I approached them . . . no wind, a very still day . . . a coincidence I thought but when I walked through, they closed behind me. I'm not the only one who's had the experience either. There was Norman Carthew too, he saw the gates open and close on a summer's day, not a breath of wind. He was quite convinced it was the ghost of Squire Kendall. There's a family tradition too, that when the master of Pelyn is to die, a phantom carriage and pair come down the drive. Well, in 1917, the then tenant heard them come, halt in front of the main door, and drive away again. My father died soon afterwards. Another coincidence, I suppose."

"I've not heard the carriage," said Frances Kendall as we talked over coffee after lunch, "but I've heard the squire riding his horse up the drive. At least, it may not have been the squire, but I certainly heard the sound of galloping hooves, and there were no horses here at the time; moreover nobody else had the authority to ride here. Nick's youngest sister, Vivian, she heard them too."

Later the Kendalls drove me along the road where the old blacksmith was reputed to have seen the ghost with his walking stick. They then took me along a minor road, which slopes down from the hamlet of Sweetshouse to the main A390, fringed by Redmoor on one side, with a distant view of Restormel Castle on the other. Late one pre-war afternoon, on this lonely stretch of road, Jill Kendall - another sister - was riding home from a day's hunting.

"Jill was riding a horse, Gary Owen, an Irish hunter, an animal of very quiet temperament. Walking along the road, going in the same direction were two women. The horse suddenly and uncharacteristically became excitable, and Jill had the utmost difficulty in getting Gary Owen past the two women. Once past, however, she turned around to apologise . . . they'd vanished! She came back to Pelyn in a great state, explaining they couldn't have simply disappeared . . . there was no gateway through which they could have slipped. She was convinced she'd seen two ghosts. One unusual thing Jill had noticed was that both women were wearing white stockings - this was in the 1930s when such things were unfashionable - could they have been from a century earlier, when stockings weren't dyed?"

NEAR PROBUS 12

AA Box Mystery

A few days after my lunch and interview with the Kendalls at Pelyn, I was back in the Lostwithiel area. The same sunny weather, but a different destination. Lanlivery, consisting of a handful of houses and an old granite church, stands on a bare, exposed shoulder of land. Twice on the journey I had lost my way and I was already nearly half-an-hour late for an appointment with Edith Watts at Snow Hill Cottage.

I enquired at the village shop.

"Mrs. Watts is expecting you, Mr. Williams."

An experience of Edith Watts's during the summer of 1966 had brought me back to the parish.

Saturday, July 9th, 1966, was a red letter day for the sailing fraternity in the South-West, and for Falmouth in particular. Thousands converged on the town for the start of the Tall Ships' race. Falmouth Bay, on a perfect summery afternoon, presented a beautiful but nostalgic sight, as a westerly wind stirred and and the vessels set sail for their eight-hundred mile voyage to The Skaw.

'It's a sight we shall never forget . . .' wrote the *Falmouth Packet* reporter aboard the *Tamar Belle*. In the midst of the armada of small boats which sailed out to see them off, the Tall Ships gave the impression of multi-storey flats amidst rows of single-storeys. In print, the *Falmouth Packet's* special colour supplement accurately anticipated the atmosphere: 'Billowing sails, the slap of canvas, the unmistakable squeak of rope against canvas and the soft pad of rope-soled shoes on wooden decks' . . . The same thrill which must have inspired mariner and Poet Laureate John Masefield when he wrote *Sea Fever* . . . 'and all I ask is a Tall Ship and a star to steer her by.'

Tallest of all was the stately *Statsraad* from Norway. Aboard the Swedish topsail schooner *Falken* was twenty year old Carl Gustaf, Sweden's Crown Prince. Also among the starters was the

Sir Winston Churchill, the first Tall Ship to be constructed in this country in the twentieth century. Built with a sense of national pride, from donations ranging from a few shillings to hundreds of pounds, the idea behind this vessel was the provision of adventure cruises for boys from all walks of life. Boys from office desks and factory floors, from colleges and schools - boys from diverse backgrounds, linked by a mutual love of the sea. A topsail schooner, the *Sir Winston Churchill* carried seven-thousand one-hundred and ten square feet of canvas.

Among the thousands of spectators, who thronged the coastline at Falmouth that summer's day, was Edith Watts, a former Chairman of Whitstable Council and the widow of a Deputy Lieutenant of Kent. Before finally settling in Cornwall, Edith Watts lived for a while, in the Bideford area of North Devon. " There I made many new friends, one of these being Councillor, Mrs. E. Brown, who became the first woman Mayor of Bideford. In January 1967, I wrote to Mrs. Brown, thanking her for her Christmas card and letter and Christmas gifts ; the usual news etc., one writes periodically to dear friends. In the letter I mentioned that last summer I had gone in a private coach to Falmouth to see the race ; this saved me the bother of driving alone in my own car and chores of parking on such a busy day. On the way, sitting in the coach, I remember we slowly passed an AA telephone kiosk beyond Probus." (Above Truro and below Grampound, Probus is a village clustered at cross-roads on the A.390).

"Opposite the AA box was a lay-by full of cars" continued Edith Watts. " As we passed, I suddenly saw Mrs. Brown standing, holding the door of the kiosk . . . and was so surprised and sorry I couldn't stop and talk to her. This I mentioned in my letter to her. I even mentioned that she was wearing blue. You can imagine my surprise when I received a letter from Mrs. Brown by return, saying how interested she was to read that I *thought I saw her* in Cornwall . . . and that she *was* in Cornwall on that day and at Probus. Seeing a telephone kiosk she had nearly asked a fellow Councillor from Bideford, (with whom she was travelling to a conference at Truro) to stop whilst she telephoned an aged aunt, who lives at Ladock, to tell her she was in the district and would try to contact her on the return journey.

" Mrs. Brown however thought better of it, as the other Councillor had various commitments and meetings that day and evening, and she did not want to upset his timetable. On the way home she did though wish very much she had tried to arrange something - but did *not* get out of the car for the telephone call, either on the way down or going back ! She was also wearing the clothes I had seen and it was the kiosk she had wanted to make a call from. Mrs. Brown herself is a Cornish woman, coming from a well-known Truro family. I'm a Northerner, from the Peak district. But what intrigues me is, supposing I had been driving my own car, of course I would have stopped when I saw Mrs. Brown . . . and then what ?"

Mrs. Watts and I talked in a room, largely furnished with Indian products. There were pistols and swords, relics of the Indian Mutiny ; statuettes and genuine Jaipur pottery in the shape of elephants. Earlier she had told me that the outside of Snow Hill Cottage had been painted white for the last five-hundred years. "This cottage and Lanlivery church tower have been landmarks for men at sea. The view from upstairs stretches from the water below Menabilly to Looe, and some nights you can see the Eddystone winking."

"Some people might think this case of yours at the AA box was one of mistaken identity " I suggested.

Edith Watts shook her head.

" I'm certain there was no question of mistaken identity. In any case, I told Mrs. Brown that the woman I saw was wearing a blue suit with white hat and gloves . . . and Mrs. Brown confirmed she was wearing those clothes."

" Did you perhaps have Mrs. Brown in your mind as the bus was travelling down the road to Falmouth ?"

" No. My mind was quite full of the Tall Ships . . . I was keenly anticipating my day at Falmouth, when suddenly I saw this woman holding the door of the kiosk. ' Good heavens, there's Mrs. Brown ! ' "

Following this exchange of letters, Mrs. Brown wrote to the Rev. Dr. G. Stephens Spinks, who was a clergyman in the West-country for several years, during which time he knew both Mrs. Brown and Mrs. Watts, telling him about the incident at the AA box.

A former editor of the world-famous *Hibbert Journal,* Dr. Spinks has given permission to quote from his letter to Mrs. Brown, written from The Vicarage, Scouthead, Oldham, Lancashire, and dated March 18th, 1967. Educated at the Universities of Oxford and London, and later elected to a Hibbert Research Studentship, Dr. Spinks's main interests have been in the border country between Philosophy and Psychology. He has contributed to overseas broadcasts of the BBC and his two recent psychological studies of religion, *The Fundamentals of Religious Belief* and *Psychology and Religion*, have been published in the United States and Holland.

"Now about your '*mystery*' in Cornwall and your own and Mrs. Watts's highly curious reactions" wrote Dr. Spinks in his letter.

"I have always thought that Mrs. Watts was a highly vivid personality. She has a series of thought-pictures, which seem to emerge every now and then about people and situations which most of us commonly forget. She has a very vivid picture in her mind of many of her friends, and no doubt you occupy a very strong place in her memory. I suggest that there is a psychological explanation of an unusual kind. As you know, we all have our ordinary level of consciousness, but in addition we all have a much more potent *unconsciousness*. Our personality is similar to that of an iceberg. About one-tenth of our nature emerges above the level of our consciousness, but below our consciousness there is the very profound depth of our unconsciousness. Our instincts are within the unconscious, and there are archetypes which create symbols and myths which embody our profoundest experience as individuals and also as members of the human race.

"Now I think in Mrs. Watts's nature there is a very active emergence of her unconsciousness. Certain personalities are associated with certain places. As she passed by the telephone kiosk on that particular day and at that particular time, her unconscious element suddenly associated the kiosk with a feeling that you were there. I think there are certain personalities which have the powers to associate people with particular places. It is possible, though this is only a suggestion, that places for certain persons have the power to stimulate their minds in a particular way. That does not apply to us all, but those who have a very vivid mind sometimes are able to rely upon their unconscious powers. It may be that you, having been near the kiosk, presented a picture in her mind when she went by that place, for it seems an undeniable fact that our minds sometimes associate personalities which are strong in our memories with actual places. I suggest that you, having been there, had left an unconscious impression upon the place, and her mind as she went by that place was stimulated by the psychological impression which you had unconsciously left upon that place.

"I am not at all sure that everybody would approve this suggestion, but I have for a long time been impressed with the fact that certain personalities in the course of history have always associated places with persons. This is an ability which is shared by people who have a very vivid psychological intuition. It may be that something of this kind, might explain your experience and Mrs. Watts's vivid apprehension. It is a remarkable gift, and one that you both seem to have possessed."

BODMIN MOOR 13

Ghost Car

" Less vast, less lofty than the moors of Devon " said the writer C. E. Vulliamy, " but infinitely more mysterious . . . " And, of course, he's right. Bodmin Moor has an indefinable magnetism, a lure that defies the average adjective.

That perceptive Westcountry character Ronald Duncan, author, poet and playwright, has felt its impact too. " The most casual visitor " he reflected, " will feel that his nose is suddenly rubbed in the past."

Take a look at the ordnance survey map : Twelve Men's Moor, so called because of the twelve tenants of Launceston Priory which owned the Moor in the thirteenth century ; Temple, where the Templars built a Norman church, in which couples were married without banns ; Stripple Stones, below Hawk's Tor, a bronze Age monument stretching one-hundred and eighty feet ; the Cheesewring, that fantastic colony of rocks, and King Doniert's Throne - the very names quicken the imagination. Lord's Waste, Black Rock, Draynes, Maiden Tor and Hard Head - places read like extracts from a novel.

This is a weird, wild world saturated in history and myth. Once the Moor was the most thickly populated area in Cornwall. Three thousand years before the stable birth at Bethlehem, ancient man encamped here. I recall the landscape painter Charles Simpson telling me : " There is an atmosphere of age in Cornwall, and the early history of man seems to brood over these hills and moors."

The A.30 snakes its way across the Moor, linking Launceston and the county town of Bodmin. Until the mid-eighteenth century there were only mediaeval tracks ; then in 1769 a turnpike road was laid and, in time, mail coaches rumbled across this " howling wilderness." Today cars, buses and lorries eat up the miles and grazing cattle live dangerously. Mary Yelland, peering out of the coach window in Daphne du Maurier's opening chapter of *Jamaica Inn*, set a century and a half ago, saw . . . " mile upon mile of bleak moorland, dark and untraversed, rolling like a desert land to some unseen horizon." The Moor, in reality, stretches twelve miles north to south, eleven miles east to west.

More than twenty years ago a motorist had a strange experience on this stretch of the A.30, at a point between Five Lanes and Bolventor, where the Jamaica Inn stands. The motorist was Patrick Humpherson of Falmouth, who roamed the world as a Merchant Navy man, and has spent most of his land life at the wheel, first as a transport driver, later as a coach driver. I'm a mixture of Irish and Scottish.

" At the time, over a score of years ago, I was ferrying vehicles from the works, Birmingham, Oxford and Coventry, and I was driving a lorry, a new one, from Birmingham to Falmouth. I'd passed through Okehampton and as it was well past eleven o'clock I didn't expect to see much traffic or sign of life, except for a few straying cattle perhaps, and because of these and the swirling mist and fog patches, I knew I should have to go cautiously. I had got beyond Five Lanes and the road was steadily climbing into dense fog with sudden clear patches.

" I hadn't been aware of anything on the road ahead, when, without warning, an old green car came from nowhere and passed me on the nearside! I had no time to brake or swerve, nor could I have done anything. It was alongside me and then gone in a flash! But in those few brief seconds I saw it as a very old open car with hood pulled back, and its four occupants were young men who were singing boisterously and half standing on their seats. The passenger in the back, furthest from me, had a hat in his hand. The car didn't have any headlights, and the only indication of lighting was an old brass lamp, the old oil type fitted between the door and windscreen. I expect I swore at these seemingly crazy idiots for passing me on the wrong side and I eased my speed, somehow half expecting something else to come out of the fog, but nothing came and I went on to Falmouth without further incident.

" The years went on, but I never got the sight of that car out of my mind. Certain details stood out very clearly. I cannot remember any engine noise but have the distinct memory of happy singing and one of the men, in his half standing position, the one nearest to me, was wearing a three-quarter length brown tweed coat.

" Then one day I came into the company of a group of coach drivers - we were in the car park at St. Ives - and there was the usual amount of leg-pulling, and this was mainly directed at one man, a most serious type who kept repeating an experience he had had the previous night. I enquired and was told he had

Rough Tor : " Did his animal instinct detect something beyond our vision and comprehension ?"
Chapter 6

Cornish Charmer Charlie Bennett, on Bossiney Lands:
"There are numerous people in North Cornwall grateful for Charlie Bennett's healing gifts." Chapter 7

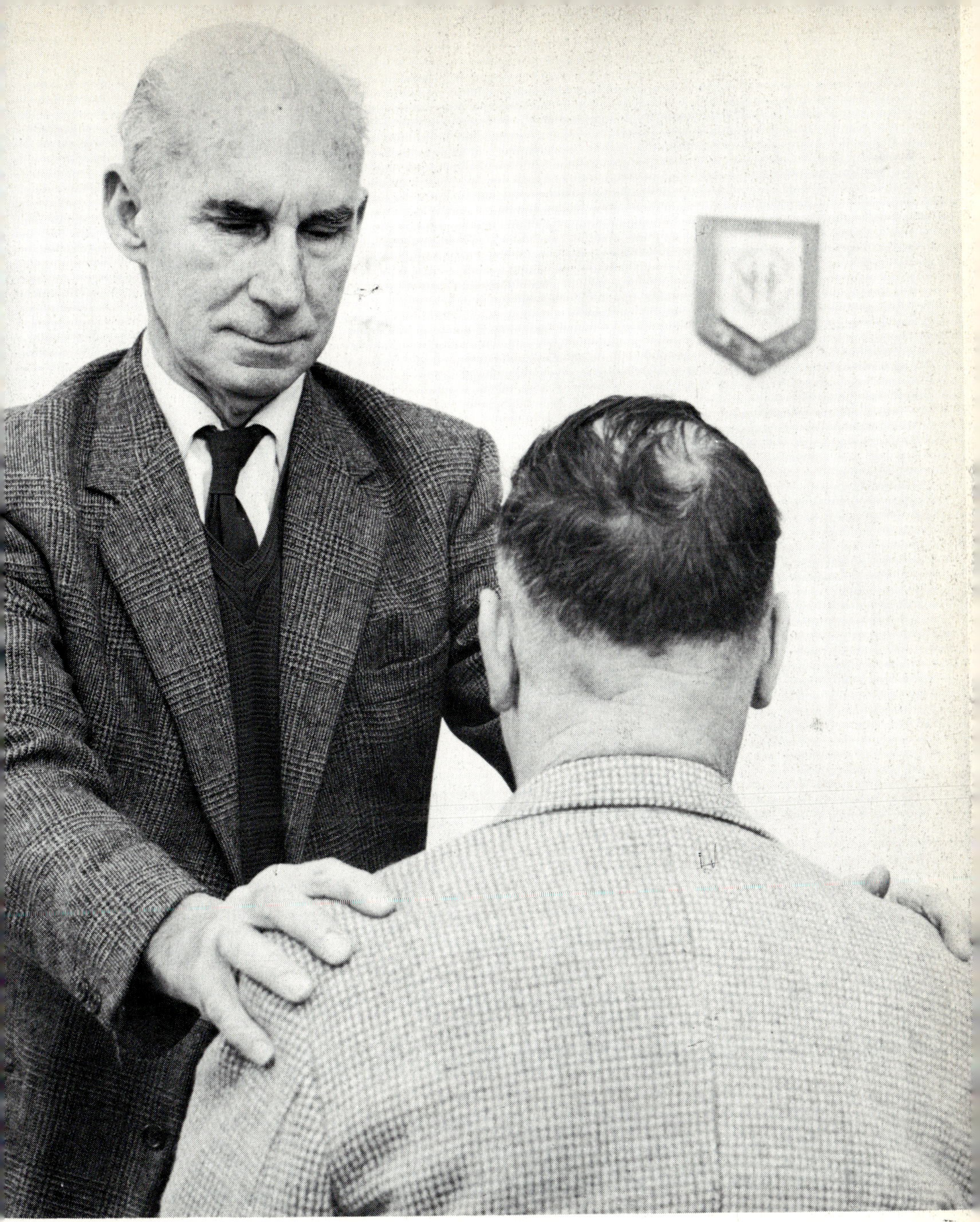

Spiritual Healer Alan Nance at St. Austell:
"Healing is uplifting for me. I experience a certain glow after treating a case." Chapter 8

UFO Student & Healer Marilyn Preston of Saltash with two ex-patients:
"It's interesting that sometimes when I've been healing we've had happenings with electrical appliances, and I'm not talking about power cuts . . ." Chapter 10

encountered a ghost car, when he was travelling from Tavistock to Liskeard. I, at once, became interested and asked a few questions and learned that this driver had encountered the same experience as me, many years before. His experience had been a few miles from where I had had mine. Before meeting this man, I had never told anyone of my encounter with the phantom car. But from this driver, I received the same description. The car and the occupants were the same I had seen."

Shortly after receiving Patrick Humpherson's account, I read of a similar encounter in *The Independent* concerning a motorist, over the border in Devon. "Flabbergasted By The Veteran Ghost Car," was the newspaper heading.

"Mr. Anthony Horne could hardly believe his eyes yesterday" wrote *The Independent* reporter, "when he read in a motoring magazine of the veteran ghost car which is reputed to haunt the roads of South Devon - he saw it himself a year ago.

"'When I read that someone had seen a spectral Daimler saloon between Modbury and Gara Bridge, I was flabbergasted,' he said.

"Mr. Horne, who lives in Westward Ho! saw it on the A.38 close to South Brent.

"'There was a slight bend,' he explained, 'and as I am a veteran car enthusiast, I was quite keen to see this one. But when I got around the corner - the road was completely empty.

"'There was no turning off on either side and it was a perfectly clear afternoon. I am the last person to believe in spooks but this was fantastic.'"

When Patrick Humpherson and I met at his home, Cra Pat, in Windsor Terrace, Falmouth, he agreed he was psychic. A silver-haired man, with penetrating blue eyes, he was wearing an open-necked shirt and talking of the supernatural as easily and as naturally as most people talk about the weather or tonight's television programmes. "But I'm not the nervy type in any way; I'm very much an out-of-doors man. All the same, I've had scores of psychic experiences." He paused for a moment. "Last night I dreamt about that veteran car, and now today you come here out of the blue, checking on some of the facts. That sort of thing's been happening all my life."

"Surely though you must get the occasional person who comes along and doesn't believe you . . . or some might say it's your imagination?"

"I couldn't care less what people think or say. Every man must think for himself, of course, but I know what I saw . . . there was no imagination."

He recalled another motoring phenomenon:

"In my coach-driving days, I was driving back from Polperro to Falmouth. A fine summer afternoon, it must have been about half-past four. I was wending my way along the road, and left Pelynt about a mile behind; the passengers were in a happy mood and I had no worries on my mind. I was approaching a bend, when suddenly, on the road past the bend - which I could see - there suddenly appeared a very large vehicle, the furniture van type. It seemed to me he came from nowhere, but there he was, and he was moving at a very fast rate. I particularly noticed the angle of the body as it heeled over to take the bend. I eased speed and expected him to come tearing around the bend, but nothing appeared. When I made the bend, there was nothing in sight, just empty road! I was puzzled. There was nowhere for a small vehicle to go, leave alone one of the size I'd seen. And *I know I saw it.*

"Now the road from Pelynt to Taphouse is very much improved, but ten years ago it was a real headache for us coach drivers. A narrow road, with lots of sharp bends, in many places with no vision of traffic coming the other way. We usually approached each bend with caution. Anyway, on this particular day, I drove on; all the passengers were still cheerful, but my thoughts were by now very mixed. I knew I had seen that van approaching. But where had it gone?

"After several miles I suddenly saw him coming towards me again on one of the most dangerous bends on that road. Fortunately, the road was a bit wider just my side of the bend. I stopped, and he came round the bend like a madman. It was impossible for him to stop when he saw me. Had I been going ahead normally, had I been only a few feet forward, there would have been a very bad crash.

"The incident was so sudden, that a hush came over the passengers. A man behind me said very quietly: 'You seemed to know he was coming round that bend,' or words to that effect. I remember replying: 'Yes, I saw him three or four miles back.'

"I had a feeling of thankfulness. I had received great help from an agency outside the scope of everyday things.

"I saw that van in the vision exactly as it was when it really did approach the bend, the angle of the body was exactly the same; and it was only the upper part of the vehicle I saw in each case, but, of course, when it did pass, I did see all of it. Not that I had time to see the driver or to take note of the number. But that driver, whoever he was, owes a lot to my vision. Without it, things would have been very different, for my passengers, and for me."

Patrick Humpherson is, in fact, a Spiritualist, though not a regular attender of Spiritualist services in Falmouth. "My attendances go in bursts. I might go regularly for a couple of years, and then not go for six months . . . that's right, I'm a bit of an individualist."

The difficulty of conversation between a Spiritualist and a non-Spiritualist is that the former often has some pretty breathtaking beliefs. Horace Leaf, for example, in his *What Spiritualism Is*, observed that "occasionally the body of a medium has entirely disappeared, only to reappear, leaving him none the worse for his remarkable experience . . ."

Patrick Humpherson in fact, claims to have seen himself.

"I was driving down into Bodmin from the A.30 - this was about fifteen years ago - off the Launceston road. I'd driven down from Birmingham. I was tired out, but I was pushing on, determined to make Falmouth without any more stops. It must have been in the early hours of the morning. I saw myself fast asleep, can remember the coat I was wearing, I've still got it somewhere . . . I saw everything from above. I was haggard, unshaven, slumped over the wheel. I must have fallen off to sleep for a matter of seconds. It couldn't have been longer, or I should have come off the road and crashed . . ."

"Do you think it was a form of dreaming or perhaps imagination?"

"Definitely not, it was too vivid for a dream, too lasting an impression. There was awe, almost fear. I'd definitely seen myself. Call it sub-conscious, call it super-conscious, call it what you will, it was a warning and it saved me. I know the difference between imagination and reality.

"You've got to remember all these unusual experiences can seldom be proved to those who've never had the experience. One doesn't know how cold water is until one jumps into it."

Patrick Humpherson's son, Geoffrey, has inherited psychic interest. "But I've not had anything like the experiences my father's had." Geoffrey has the same blue penetrating eyes. He practises Yoga. "I suppose the Beatles helped my interest in the mystical." He first saw strange figures at the age of twelve. Then, three years ago, in the company of friends, he was conscious of a figure. Nobody else could see it, so he described it. " That's one of my guides," a medium told him. " As far as I can remember, we were only talking about everyday things when this figure appeared to me." Geoffrey pointed to the wall opposite us. " Another time I was sitting where you're sitting now, and I saw this face build up on the wall : an aristocratic type, with a black moustache ; French, I'd say . . ."

" What about your father's psychic experiences ?"

" Fantastic, aren't they ?"

" Wouldn't you say, though, that your father's imaginative ?"

" Oh, yes, he's imaginative. But he analyses. He'll go to a service, and then come back here, and start working things out. He just doesn't blindly accept things. He works things out for himself."

POLZEATH 14

Strange Events

Eleanor Inglefield is a Roman Catholic. Her mother was Delius's youngest sister - there were fourteen children - her father was a brigadier. She was born at Aldershot in 1907. " The first things I can remember are bands and the tramp of marching feet. My father had weird ideas regarding girls' schools, and I was never allowed to go to one. ' Hotbeds of vice,' my father used to say darkly. As we trailed from garrison town to garrison town, elderly ladies were found to give me lessons . . . each usually depreciated the methods of her predecessor and took me back to the beginning to set me on the right path !

" Do I regret my education or lack of it ? No. It was great fun.

"I served in the FANY for seven years; have always been enchanted by Cornwall. I've written several articles on Cornwall . . . and, when required, I do night duty at the East Cornwall Hospital, at Bodmin . . . nothing very exciting, really . . . " Now she lives at Rock, a sheltered spot by the Camel Estuary, but until 1963, she lived at Penglaze, a cottage at New Polzeath.

Penglaze, a bungalow with slated, sloping roof and veranda, overlooks Pentire Glaze Haven - Baby Bay, as the locals call it - and a tiny beach. Away to the right is Breakneck Cavern ; above, National Trust land stretches away to the Rumps. To the left are Stepper Point and Trevose Head, where at night, the lighthouse makes its regular patterns. Tamarisks shelter one side of the cottage ; on the other, only reedy marshland stands between the building and sloping shoulder of the valley.

" A week after moving in I was going to bed in my bedroom, next to the small sitting room, when suddenly I was aware of someone else sharing the cottage with me. A man was moving slowly, leisurely, about next door. The movements were not those of a man stealthily anxious not to be heard ; I got the impression they were the movements of somebody in his own home. I sat on the edge of the bed, following the sound of the movements with puzzled concentration. They were the movements of an elderly, methodical man: the sounds suggested he was doing the sort of thing he did every night . . . the pushing back of chairs, the drawing back of curtains; I could hear the swish and the rattle of curtain chains. Then, in the same, slow deliberate way, he crossed the room and knocked his pipe out against the fireplace. After that there was silence.

"I didn't go into the room for about three minutes . . . it was a matter of plucking up courage to go and investigate. The room was completely empty . . . nothing had been touched or moved . . . there was no sign of pipe ash in the fireplace. But I still had the distinct impression I had just heard an elderly man putting the room to rights for the night. Oddly enough, after my first feeling of nervousness, I didn't feel in the least frightened. I felt the presence to be altogether friendly and perfectly harmless. Though I lived in that cottage for another eight and a half years, I never heard my old visitor again."

Eleanor Inglefield did however have further unusual experiences at Penglaze. "It was shortly before I left. It was the night Telstar was being televised for the first time. Having no television of my own, I went up to a friend in New Polzeath and saw the programme from there. As you'll no doubt remember, it came through nearly two hours late, and it was past one o'clock in the morning when I started for home. As I came down the rough path leading into the valley, I was surprised to see the cottage flooded with light. It looked as if there was a floodlight in the garden. I stood there staring. Then it came to me that what I, in fact saw, were the headlights of a car. Night fishermen often came down the valley and left their cars near my gate. Any moment I expected to hear a car starting up. Nothing happened. The light just burnt steadily on, everything silent. I was almost at the foot of the path when, without warning, the light went out. I stared round looking for a car . . . but there was no car. There were no fishermen in the valley, either. The place was utterly deserted, except for myself. Unlike my old man, I did see the light more than once. I saw the light twice more in the remaining eight months there . . . both times coming down the same path late at night . . . it all occurred after my mother's death. She lived there with me for several years . . . she loved the place."

"Do you think these lights might have been connected with your mother's death?"

"I've always thought so."

"Or do you think it might have been your imagination?"

"It might - and I only say might - have been imagination on the second and third occasions, but I'm certain it wasn't my imagination on the first occasion. I wasn't anticipating anything supernatural. I was thinking in terms of the headlights of a car. Even the second and third time, I'm by no means prepared to admit it was just imagination. The lighthouse? Oh, no. That's a red light, and anyway it wouldn't have had the width and penetration of the light I saw* . . . the whole of the cottage was lit."

"Are you psychic?"

"No, just a little sensitive. Never seen a ghost in my life; wish I had. My mother, though, she was psychic. I clearly remember, about two years before her death, one evening I was in the kitchen, cooking supper, and she called out suddenly . . . there was something wrong. I hurried into the sitting room; mother was standing by the French window.

"'Has he come round to the back?'" she asked.

"Who?" I asked blankly.

"'I think it's Bob,' my mother said. 'He tapped the window, the way he always does. I opened the door at once, but he wasn't there.'

"I went out immediately, walked around the bungalow. There was nobody in sight. But I was a bit disturbed. I knew something my mother didn't know: brother Bob had cancer and was doomed. He died about nine months later."

We talked at Daymer Bay in the afternoon. There were only three cars parked; in summer there would have been hundreds. Two dogs hared across the beach, their paw marks patterning the smooth, virgin sand. There was activity on the water. In the season, like a lagoon, it becomes a paradise for sailing and water ski-ing. On the other side lay Padstow, the safest harbour on the North Coast, and the setting of the Hobby Horse Festival every May Day. St. Petroc went to Padstow in the sixth century. Around his church an area of sanctuary was created for criminals; and once inside, they were safe from the law, at least until the Reformation.

"Yes, my mother was definitely psychic" Eleanor Inglefield continued. "Personally, I've had one or two strange experiences.

*Recent occupants confirmed this opinion. "The Trevose light never reaches here on that scale," said a Cambridge GP, staying at Penglaze.

" Back in 1945, I was stationed in Ilfracombe, in North Devon. I had a passion for walking and I decided to climb the Hangman Hills . . . there are two of them 'The Lesser' and 'The Greater Hangman.' The climb from the village of Coombe Martin is about half-an-hour, fairly fast climbing. The village soon drops from sight under the shoulder of the hill and the climber is alone with wind and sun and glorious scenery. Leaving the lesser hill on my left, I began to approach the main summit, and, with surprise, noticed that the grass ended quite abruptly . . . a circle of stoney ground crowned the top of the hill. I remember thinking, in a disinterested way, that the altitude was surely not as high as that. At any rate, I crossed the boundary of grass and stoney ground and started the last ascent. Everything was alright until I saw the small cairn of stones. I wish I could describe the shape, but I cannot. It was roughly the same structure as a Cornish cross, but very roughly. My first thought was that some child had been playing with the stones, but I knew that was ridiculous ; no child would play in this lonely place. Then I saw the second cairn, slightly larger than the first, and just behind it. It was at that point that the nightmare began to manifest itself. There were hundreds of things, varying from a few inches in height to some, seven feet high. They were all about me . . . and the terror they inspired was something I shall never forget. I knew I was utterly at the mercy of something that not only could, but would, annihilate me in a flick of time . . . something that resented me being there.

" I cannot pretend to understand what it was I faced on that brilliant day in June, 1945. All I know is, it had tremendous power, and I knew, moreover, that the thing I feared could only be seen by me in the shape of those stone cairns. They were the symbols that reflected the reality just as St. John could only see the truth of God in weird beasts ; not that this was the truth of God . . . very much the reverse. Another odd thing is that the top of the hill had gone ; I was facing a huge stoney plain, stretching as far as the eye could see. I had stepped into another dimension with a vengeance. Suddenly, I thought of the Lord's Prayer - it was the only thing I could think of - slowly and aloud I began to recite it. The rigidity left my limbs and I could move. I turned back. I was quite near the grass. The cairns were still about me, but they seemed to have receded. I began to walk. I knew - God knows how - that once I crossed on to the green grass I would be safe. As I walked, I was aware of something behind me, but I dare not look around. As I stepped on to the green turf, I knew that which followed had halted . . . it could not cross the boundary.

" As I hurried down the hill, I looked back. The stoney hill crest was there . . . but nothing else . . . "

Eleanor Inglefield's other recollection also belongs to her service days.

" One week-end I went up from Bulford Camp on Salisbury Plain, where I was then stationed, to visit some friends who were at OCTU in Windsor. I hadn't booked any accommodation; but before I started, a girl who worked as a clerk in the company office had mentioned a hotel, Thorplea, in Egham. Any name being better than none, I got off the Royal Blue at Egham, and was directed to Thorplea.

" Thorplea had once been somebody's lovely old country house, but it had become rather shabby over the years, and the gardens around it were beautiful, but neglected. The old place had a vague feeling of familiarity, but the feeling wasn't strong enough to be impressive. The manageress, after a slight hesitation, said she had one room vacant, if I didn't mind being at the top of the house. It was an ordinary, very comfortable room. Looking around, I congratulated myself on my good fortune . . .

" That night I met my friends for supper and got back to Thorplea about ten. I went to bed and was soon asleep. A dream crash woke me, and I sat up. The first thing I smelt was hay. The next thing I was aware of was, that instead of bed clothes, my hands rested on rough bales of hay. A new awareness rushed in on me. I knew that somebody had deliberately thrust me into the loft, and the sound that had woken me was the sound of the trap door being slammed. It was by now, as I knew, bolted on the other side. I was a prisoner. What devilry had gone before, I had no idea. I only knew that whoever it was who had placed me here intended my death. I could see the window, where it had been when I went to bed, slightly to my left. I got to my feet, groped my way between bales of hay, guiding myself with my hands, and looked out. The scene was much the same as when I had looked out from the hotel window : cobbled courtyard surrounded by derelict stables. But now the cobbles were unchoked by weeds, and there was a carriage resting on its shafts. I examined the drop, from window to ground. It must have been seventy to eighty feet . . . and nothing but stone on which to fall. I have no head for heights now, and I had the same vertigo then. There was, however, only one hope of escape, slender though the chance was. I had to slide down the drain pipe. I climbed out on to the window sill and sat there, feeling sick. I knew I hadn't a chance in a millon. Oddly enough, the thing that was uppermost in my mind was the fear that if I fell, *they* would think I had committed suicide . . . and I was passionately anxious this should not happen. It even dominated my terror.

"Once again the Lord's Prayer came to my mind. I began to recite it. Suddenly I felt a cold wind in my face. I was sitting outside the hotel bedroom window, my legs dangling over the sill. I threw myself backwards into the bedroom. I'd been within an ace of death."

ST. ISSEY 15

Violent Forces

Westward beyond Wadebridge, the road climbs like a C going the wrong way. Something over two miles on, the signpost to Padstow appears on the right-hand side. But Padstow was not my destination.

Twenty minutes later I was sitting in front of Canon Elias Truscott, the Vicar of St. Issey. He was seated at his desk. A typewriter, with half a page already typed, had been pushed to one side. We were in the study of his rectory, a Georgian building in its own grounds. St. Issey is on this twisting road which joins Wadebridge and Padstow. On Easter Sunday, 1967, lightning struck the church tower here. Fragments of the pinnacle were thrown as far as eighty yards ; the church roof and those of neighbouring cottages were holed ; a headstone in the churchyard was shattered. This was history repeating itself. In 1869 it was damaged by lightning, and had to be reconstructed. Who said lightning never strikes twice ?

The church, almost totally rebuilt around 1870, has a late fourteenth century reredos, which Dr. Pevsner considered to be by " The Master of St. Endellion ;" it has five panels of dark Caraclewse stone and twenty angels. Apart from the Ring O'Bells, a popular inn, the church and vicarage, St. Issey is little more than a cluster of slate houses. It has grown up in pleasant countryside ; narrow lanes wind down to the estuaries of the Camel and Little Petherick. This is basically unspoilt, uncommercialised Cornwall. But my appointment coincided with a misty day ; insidious patches, robbing part of the landscape, gave the impression of an incomplete jigsaw puzzle with bits and pieces missing.

Our interview, however, had nothing to do with lightning or this parish.

The Canon was studying four typewritten sheets. " These are the last copies I have. It was such an experience, that I felt a written report was necessary. It is such a fantastic story, one might have asked later on : ' Did it all really happen ? ' "

Earlier in the month, I had written to the Bishop of Truro asking him if any of the Cornish clergy had been called upon to cope with supernatural forces ? The Bishop had advised me to contact Canon Truscott.

" I even went to the extent of having them signed by the people who had been involved. This is the genuine account" said the Canon, holding the faintly yellowed sheets in his right hand. " More than twenty years ago it all happened, but I wrote this account only a matter of days after it was all over. What's here is the authentic record.

" I'm prepared to let you take these notes, provided you return them to me, and provided you don't divulge the name of the family concerned. Though they've now left Cornwall, I prefer them to remain anonymous.

" At the end of the week," Canon Truscott confessed, " we were at our wits' end. I remember the father coming to me at the end of it all, and saying : ' If we hadn't you to cling to, I don't know what would have happened to us. I never want to live through another such week.' "

The following, culled from Canon Truscott's notes, concerns the parish of Rame, where he was once vicar. The most easterly parish in Cornwall, Rame and next-door Maker spread themselves over a brace of peninsulas facing Plymouth Sound and the English Channel. Beaches there are sandy and inviting, but bathing is dangerous. Rame itself is a hamlet. The parish church has a thin Norman tower and spire, something akin to St. Endellion. " A delightful, crude little church," somebody has called it, "looking like a rustic's attempt to copy Sheviock, spire and all." There was a Norman church on the site, parts of which remain. Inside, broomsticks, nailed vertically to the bench ends, act as candlesticks.

On October 27th, 1941, the Rector was called to baptise an infant baby of Mr. and Mrs. H., who lived in a cottage near the rectory. The baby later became ill, was removed to hospital, but soon afterwards died of encephalitis.

Four months later, on Saturday, February 28th, Mr. Truscott visited the cottage to press, as he had done on several previous occasions, for the baptism of the younger of the two remaining children. There were two boys, one aged nine, the other between the age of two and three. Both parents were out, but the grandmother and elder boy were at home. Frightened and overwrought, the old woman began to tell the Rector of things moving about : chiefly articles connected with dead baby. These strange movements occurred from about 3.30 in the afternoon, the time of the child's death, and increased in violence as the day wore on. Initially sceptical, the Rector, on reflection, realised the old woman was genuinely upset; moreover he could see no reason for the invention of such a tale. The mother of the dead child, he remembered, had been overstrained since the death four months ago; during pregnancy she had been blitzed out of her old home, even confinement had taken place during an air-raid. The Rector prayed with the grandmother and arranged for the younger boy to be brought for baptism next day, Sunday afternoon. The parents and children, however, failed to appear at the church for the service.

Meanwhile manifestations continued to increase in the cottage. An appeal was made to the Rector for help and comfort; he was sent for on the Tuesday night, but was away, and was unable to go to the cottage until the Wednesday morning. The father of the children, a soldier, serving at the nearby fort, had been given compassionate leave. At first, he too had been sceptical, but by the time of the Rector's arrival on that Wednesday morning he had been convinced. Inanimate objects had moved before his eyes.

Neither parent actually saw the ghost of their dead daughter, but both said they were conscious of her presence. Objects, associated with her short life, became violent in movement. The Rector again suggested baptism, and, that same afternoon in Rame Church, in the presence of the parents, the ceremony was performed. After the service, taking a quantity of holy water with him, the Rector revisited the cottage for a blessing rite. Beginning his blessing in the sitting room, he was immediately interrupted. A saucepan of water on the scullery stove was thrown down violently and water was streaming all over the floor. Then, with loud crashing, a chair fell into the sitting room fender.

On returning to the Rectory, Canon Truscott attempted to telephone the Bishop at Truro, but he was unable to get through; he did, however, succeed in contacting the Archdeacon, who suggested some responsible people should be taken to watch the cottage. On contacting the local Army unit, two sergeants and three privates were detailed for the job.

By this time the focus of attention had shifted from articles connected with the dead infant to those which had connection with the older boy. The Rector now suspected a strong association of fear between this older child and his grandmother.

Whenever the five soldiers, the father and the rector were in the house, nothing unusual happened. At the Rector's suggestion, all seven men went outside the cottage; a sergeant, unsuspected by the boy or his grandparent inside, watching through a window, saw the boy lift a table. On being questioned, the nine-year-old confessed he had been heaved from the settee and impelled to lift the table. Two soldiers watched in the sitting room, while grandmother and grandson were in the scullery, and *vice versa*. Later, both soldiers signed statements to the effect they had seen unaccountable incidents : a kettle had twice been thrown down - no one had been near it - they had seen the boy throw a tin into a corner, whereupon the tin, of its own accord, flew back across the room. After close observation, the military contingent became convinced the disturbances and the older boy were related. While the boy was in the house, crockery was propelled and smashed, chairs and tables were lifted by invisible hands and hurled with great force. The boy had utmost difficulty at meal times when food refused to stay on his plate. The mother, one day, when polishing the floor, had to get up and hold a picture - such were its vibrations - on another occasion, a cupboard, flying open, hit her on the head, and slammed to with such power that its hinges were broken. In preparing meals, Mrs. H kept the boy out of the house because immediately on his reappearance things started happening. If he hung up his cap and coat, they were flung to the ground.

On the Thursday night, none of the family were able to sleep. Beds bounced up and down. Ornaments and crockery continued to fly around the cottage ; the wireless was overturned. The following morning, mother and son had a nasty experience in one of the bedrooms: a wardrobe came towards them three times, contents were swept from a dressing table, a tallboy jumped, and a cot leapt at them as they left the room. On the staircase, Mrs. H was struck in the back by an airborne suitcase. Disturbances became so aggressive that, on this Friday morning, the boy was sent to the fort with his father, and remained there for a meal - Mrs. H being too agitated to do any cooking. Nothing however happened in the boy's absence ; nothing unusual occurred at the fort either.

By this time it had become clear that the boy - and not his grandmother - was the link. The Rector, on his next visit to the cottage, therefore decided to make a test ; he positioned the boy in the scullery, telling him he would be in the next room, looking out of the window, which meant no view of the boy in the scullery. Four times the Rector was called to the scullery ; four times the boy insisted the table had leapt at him. Canon Truscott then made further, more precise experimentation, by standing the boy on two flowers on the linoleum, a position from which the boy could touch neither the table nor the bath-tub (two objects which had been remarkably active during this nightmare week), nor the mantelpiece behind, nor the gas stove against the fourth wall. The grandmother was stationed in the sitting room, both parents were outside the cottage, for the Rector was keen to determine whether the magnetic force was on one particular side or all round. Watching through a chink in the door, Canon Truscott, in his own words, "saw the gate-legged table rise squarely with speed and force, stop suddenly at a height of about two feet, and then drop with terrific force." But he also observed activity by the boy : the lifting of a mat, the only object within reach.

The boy, on being questioned, confessed he had moved the mat ; whereupon the Rector took him into the garden and made the following observations :

(a) His father was liable to immediate arrest for obtaining extra leave under false pretences.

(b) His mother was quite likely to have a nervous breakdown.

(c) The boy had been found guilty in three cases : lifting the table, witnessed by the sergeant ; throwing the tin, witnessed by the soldiers ; and now the lifting of the mat, witnessed by the Rector himself.

(d) The whole thing had gone beyond a joke - the boy had been in tears for most of the day.

(e) What was the point of wearing out his parents, making fools of them and the Rector, defying the policeman, who had now been called in, and the soldiers ?

The Rector called the father, explained that the boy had begun to confess, and suggested his son should now be induced to confess everything. The boy, though pressed, refused to admit anything beyond the three cases observed ; he appeared anxious to help, but his agitated, tear-stained condition made further questioning impossible.

It was at this point, a decision was made to call in the family doctor. ("something we should have done earlier," Canon Truscott reflected, "but you must remember we were up against something none of us had encountered before in our lives"). Before the arrival of the GP the mother, unwilling to accept the possibility that her elder son had deceived everybody, made one final, desperate experiment. Tying the boy's hands behind his back with a green belt, she sent him into the scullery. Mother and grandmother stood and watched as pots, pans and chairs danced before him. The Rector and the father, coming into the scullery, were confronted by a terrible wreckage.

At 8.15, the doctor arrived, made a thorough examination, pronounced the boy physically fit, and said mentally he could neither be certified nor even recommended as a voluntary patient. On hearing the details of the past week, the doctor sent the boy and his mother from the room, and told the two men that nothing they had told him was impossible for the boy. He recalled an instance in a certain hospital, when he had seen a table leave fourteen doctors, sitting at it, and pass through a doorway with only the fraction of an inch to spare.

The doctor advised the removal of the boy from his present environment. He appeared more concerned about the condition of the mother who, in his opinion, was on the verge of a serious break-down.

The Rector, bearing a medical certificate from the GP, went to the fort, where he was sympathetically received. The earlier military scoffing had disappeared. The authorities gave the boy's father overnight leave, plus a week-end pass, for the purpose of taking his son to Leeds to his grandparents - and for further observation.

On the boy's departure, disturbances at the cottage ceased, and, soon after, the entire family left Rame.

"The remarkable thing about the whole case," observed Canon Truscott, "is the violent noise and force with which things were moved . . . it still remains to be discovered whether it was a case of possession, magnetism, hypnotism or some force unknown."

Nicholas Kendall in front of the Squire's portrait at Pelyn, Lostwithiel:
"There's a family tradition too that when the master of Pelyn is to die, a phantom carriage and pair come down the drive." Chapter 11

AA Box between Probus & Tresillian:
"I suddenly saw Mrs. Brown, standing, holding the door of the kiosk."

Chapter 12

Eleanor Inglefield, great-niece of Delius: "I threw myself backwards into the bedroom. I'd been within an ace of death." Chapter 14

Alan Sandry showing the spot near Little Petherick :
" It was about three and a half feet tall, certainly under four feet I'd say : a faceless thing with short legs and it walked a jogging motion."
Chapter 16

LITTLE PETHERICK 16

Ghostly Meetings

Beyond St. Issey lies Little Petherick, a village as small as its name implies. Situated on the same A.389, two and a half miles from the port of Padstow, Little Petherick is set at a creek of the River Camel, within a nature reserve and bird sanctuary. Like St. Issey, this parish is relatively unscarred.

Just after the village, one drizzly, dull Sunday morning, I turned sharply left and arrived at the Rosehill Country Club. Standing in four acres of ground, it is run by Frederick Paxton and his German-born wife, Edda. In the old world club bar, over a couple of sherries, I talked to Frederick Paxton and Alan Sandry, one of the club members, about their ghostly meetings last summer. Frederick Paxton, an ex-Secretary for the Farmers' Union, in Derbyshire, has been running Rosehill since 1959. Alan Sandry is a native ; a farmer, he has over three-hundred acres at Trevisker, south-east of Padstow.

" It's refreshing to meet someone who's not cynical," said Frederick Paxton, standing behind the bar. " When Alan and I appeared on television after our little experience, people thought it was a gimmick, a publicity stunt for the Rosehill Country Club ; but it wasn't, I can assure you . . . we merely told David Mudd about what we'd seen . . . no invention at all."

" It all began because my car had broken down," Alan Sandry explained. He and I were sitting on stools on the customers' side of the counter. It is a bar with beams and plenty of character : a yard of ale above the counter, oil paintings and cutlasses on the walls, a coachman's horn and a warming pan. " As the car was out of action," Alan Sandry continued, " I had to walk over the fields for a drink. I walk instinctively on the left-hand side, a legacy of boyhood, I suppose, when I stuck to the left . . . imprinted on my mind I suppose. It was Friday evening, July 14th, to be precise. I'd had three or four pints here in the bar and was on my way back home. It must have been around eleven o'clock when I met this something. It was something unusual, and I was uncertain what it was. This figure was poking into the hedge. First, I thought it was a courting couple. It was aware of me, and then it vanished. I just couldn't make it out.

"Then on July 16th, the Sunday evening that would be, I was here again, and left after a few drinks, took the same route back home on foot, and there it was, lying in the middle of the road. On seeing me, it turned its head towards me, then trotted towards the hedge, where it disappeared."

"Were you perhaps thinking you might encounter this object again that night? Some people would say you imagined it this second time . . ."

Alan Sandy smiled: "I'll tell you what I was thinking about. I was thinking about some Vickers' shares and what a rotten price they were! And I wasn't drunk. I'd hardly have been thinking about stocks and shares if I'd been one over the eight. It was a better light this time, and I got a better view of it. It was about three and a half feet tall, certainly under four feet. I'd say: a faceless thing, with short legs and it walked with a jogging motion.

"I saw it a third time on July 21st. I know these dates and times, because I jotted down some notes immediately I got back to the farm. This was around 1.55. I'd deliberately left it late, wondering if it would be possible to see if later in the night. The other occasions had been a lot earlier. I made my usual approach, and there it was in perfect shape."

Prior to our conversation, Frederick Paxton had shown me the area in question. Later Alan did the same. It is a branch of the main A.389, part of the old road, shaped, in fact, like the climb out of Wadebridge: a C the wrong way around; it's now used as a lay-by or a short cut.

"I got within ten or twelve paces of it." Alan Sandry went on, "and tried to converse with it; said I was a Christian and wanted to know if I could help. This time it was shrouded, nothing visible except for the grey robes, and I couldn't see through it. It was a bright moonlight, and it appeared to be solid, but it didn't cast a shadow. Yes, I admit I was really frightened this time; it seemed taller, four and a half feet, perhaps, up to my shoulder, I'd say. It had a slight stoop and tottered about. Again it disappeared into this hedge.

"The next time I came in here, I said to Fred: 'You know, I think I've seen a ghost.' Well, Fred said he'd like to see it, too. So we agreed we'd go up to the old road together."

" We weren't able to set out until nearly midnight," Frederick Paxton recalled. " I'd been busy with grills down in the dining room. And before we got to this old stretch of the road, Alan turned around and said : ' Stop your loose change rattling and put your cigarette out.' Suddenly, there it was . . . more or less in the middle of the road. Alan whipped round : ' Did you see it ?' ' My God, yes, I did,' I replied. He, she or it was just as Alan had described. It was obviously scratching or doing something with its hands . . ."

" Could it possibly have been an animal ?" I interrupted.

" No, it straightened itself up in the way an ordinary human being would, but though there were hands and legs, no face was visible. Then it sidled across into the hedge of the left-hand side. We looked into the hedge, but couldn't find any clues, nothing seemed disturbed, when suddenly, back on the road behind us, it appeared again. This time its pace changed, no sidling . . . a darting movement this time, it dashed away from the middle of the road and disappeared back into the hedge. We investigated again, but still no sign of it. I've been back there six or seven times, but I've seen nothing."

" Have you got any theories ?"

Frederick Paxton sipped his drink : " Well, they say there was a wayside grave in the old copse, near that bit of road. It might have had something to do with that."

Alan Sandry came back into the conversation.

" That bit of road, you know, was part of the old priest's path that stretched from Padstow to Bodmin. It was certainly something like a monk-like figure. And since we appeared on television, I understand a former district nurse has admitted that she's seen a similar figure in that area. And only a few weeks ago somebody I know, who previously had been very sceptical on the subject of ghosts, said he'd seen the same thing."

" I think until you experience something like this you are inclined to be cynical," reflected Frederick Paxton. " I remember the night Alan said : ' Either I'm going silly or I've seen a ghost.' I've always had an open mind on the subject of the supernatural, but now I'm quite convinced. The sight of this little figure is deeply imprinted on my mind . . . no question of being drunk or imagining the thing."

" Have you seen it again ?" I asked Alan Sandry.

" Yes. I saw it on a fifth occasion. And another time I took somebody there, and we saw a movement of some kind, but I didn't count that as seeing it. Five times I've seen it quite clearly, and there's been no doubt at all in my mind."

WITHIEL 17

Clairvoyant

" As a child, you were very shy, but you wrestled with this shyness and overcame it. Your years as a schoolmaster must have helped you. But you've had to wrestle with a lot of inner conflicts too. You've had a great many decisions to make, especially in the last five years . . . I'd say your life has undergone many changes."

The woman in sweater, slacks and sandals was holding my right hand. " You're right handed, are you ?" She was intently studying contours of the palm : my first experience of clairvoyance in action.

An advertisement in the miscellaneous column of *The Cornish Guardian* had brought me to Withiel. " Lady Clairvoyant, Psychemtrist, Palm and Hand Reading by appointment only." The old farmhouse lay at the foot of a narrow road which climbs to Withiel, a village, beneath St. Columb Down, conspicuous on the strength of its granite three-stage church tower. We sat in a room with beamed ceiling, an open pointed stone fireplace with a cloam oven. Three circular prints dominated the walls. I sat on a Regency striped chair. A desk stood in a corner. The view from the window led onto a small garden, beyond which sprawled the farmyard. Fine rain was falling from a sombre, grey sky.

Elizabeth Dorothy - " But always known as Betty " - Lukey has been practising clairvoyance for more than twenty years. " Until this year, though I'd done it only for friends and charity. Then somebody suggested I should do it professionally to supplement my income. I had a bit of a conscience about taking money at first . . . but as you say I suppose the labourer is worthy of his hire. Anyway the first time I inserted an advertisement in *The Cornish Guardian* I had as many as twenty-two phone calls.

Once more the character and the geographical direction of my journey had changed. Again I had travelled back inland, first onto the main Wadebridge road, then deeper into the countryside. As with spiritual healing, I have had no inhibition about including clairvoyance here. Has not clairvoyance long been regarded as a form of divination, and associated with qualities attributed to mystics and religious seers?

"Knowledge of information not necessarily known to any other person, obtained independently of ordinary channels of perceiving and reasoning," was how *The Encyclopaedia Britannica* defined clairvoyance. *Chambers* referred to "the extrasensory perception of objects or objective events" and my old faithful, *The Concise Oxford* gave fourteen words: "Faculty of seeing mentally what is happening or exists out of sight; exceptional sight."

People everywhere are curious about the future, interested in the prospects of a love affair or a business venture. Time was when sooth-sayers, fortune-tellers and kindred spirits were consulted by rulers of kingdoms on strategy in battle or policy-making in peacetime. In Greece men and women, with the power of prediction, were valued members of society and were given special training. In ancient Rome, there was a college of augury, whose business it was to ascertain whether the Gods were in favour or against proposed plans. The augur usually pitched his tent on the summit of a hill, asked the Gods for a sign, and, with head covered, awaited their reply. The appearance of birds or signs in the heavens, like lightning or rain, were interpreted.

History is studded with examples. Queen Boadicea released a hare from her clothes and drew a favourable omen from the way it ran. The Babylonians examined the liver of a sacrificed sheep and drew their conclusions. In some European countries the shoulder-blades of animals were examined; our presentday practice of breaking the wish-bone of a chicken at the dinner table is of course a legacy of such custom. Astrology, a popular form of peering into the future, is five-thousand years old. There is even belief - by some - that the spirits of the dead may be conjured up to give information to the living. In the Bible, we read the story of Saul visiting the woman of Endor who called up for him the spirit of Samuel.

Earlier Betty Lukey had held my watch in her hands, had used it as a means of uncovering the past and probing the future. Her knowledge of my past was certainly accurate, her assessment of my personality too. I had always thought of clairvoyants as brunettes. Betty Lukey is a blonde. I had somehow visualised a strange witch-like woman peering into a crystal. There was no crystal. In fact she practises four methods. "Holding an object, a ring or a watch, something personal. Then there's reading cards or reading palms and hands. And there's the method of just meeting people, when I'm tuned in with somebody, things come out, you get to the subconscious ; they may not be thinking about something but it comes out ; obviously, though, if they were thinking about it, it would be much easier . . . much easier. One picks up something in the ether. We don't realise how much is in the atmosphere . . . it's a matter of tuning in to vibrations . . . transmissions. When I decided to do this professionally. I *knew* this was the room in which I had to work. Don't ask me why. We're really back to atmosphere. This inward peace I feel here. That must be it."

Betty Lukey was born just outside Cornwall, at Manamead, Plymouth. " After seeing *Peter Pan* I had a recurring dream in which I used to open my bedroom window and fly out into the night. Up and up I used to float through the stars and then I seemed weightless and just stayed suspended with arms outstretched, gazing down on Plymouth Hoe. The scene is as vivid now as it was all those years ago. Oh, the wonderful feeling of freedom. How I hated waking up !"

" Being a clairvoyant, doesn't that make people think you're different . . . that you're not quite one of them?" A long pensive silence.

" In the old days I would blurt things out. But now I discriminate. You know when and to whom you talk. There was an occasion at school . . . telling a friend something and she didn't believe me. It was a rather shattering experience because until then I had assumed everybody shared the same kind of vision."

" When did the realisation really come - to you - that you were different from others, and that you possessed special gifts ?" A pin silence.

" I must have been about fifteen. We were living in Surrey, a place called Chantersluer near Leigh. It was the first time I'd lived in the country. Part of the house was fourteenth century, and I never liked going into the kitchen alone at night. My mother had gone to London, and I was sitting in the drawing room : suddenly the dog had jumped off my lap and was trying to get under the sofa, all hackles up. A monk was standing in the doorway . . . head and shoulders only. I was absolutely terrified. 'please, God, take this thing away!' I tried to call out to my sister who was upstairs, bu I had no voice. Then I made the sign of the cross, and he vanished! I rushed upstairs and told my sister what I'd seen. ' It was the cheese,' she said, ' you ate too much.' And I kept this cheese thing. I didn't want to admit this monk business. About three years later, an American woman, she'd either stayed there before or might even have lived there, gave us some of the background. Apparently part of the house had been a monastery. There was something very evil about the place, and the villagers decided to do something about it . . . part of it was burnt down.

" When I was still quite young, I fell in love. At this stage I found that I was able to see into the future - our future - I could hear strange sounds. I later learned they were sirens. I could see him having to go away . . . I was foreseeing the war and didn't realise it. When the time came - ten years later - for this affair to end, and I knew it must end . . . I sat down to write a letter that was to end it all . . . probably one of the most important letters I've written in all my life. The words came tumbling out, sentence followed sentence without a pause. I had a strong feeling that I'd written this letter somewhere before.

" This feeling of having done something before, or having been there before, has kept cropping up. When the door of this house first opened, and I stepped inside, I *knew* this was to be an important place for me, knew it instinctively, immediately. Then I came across some fiction I'd written as a schoolgirl . . . this place, the farmhouse, the farmyard, the garden . . . it was all written down. I'd been here before, in my mind."

" As a clairvoyant, you must have had some strange experiences. Is there anything which stands out especially in your memory ?"

" A few years ago, I had ten friends in, there was also my husband and myself : twelve of us for a table turning session. We sat round a table with the letters of the alphabet set in a circle, in the centre of which was a glass tumbler turned upside-down ; we each rested a tip of a finger on the glass, sat in silence and awaited results after asking ' Is anybody there ?' After a while the glass began to move, and various messages were spelt out. At this stage, my Finnish maid, Margot, peered through a portion of the stained glass window in the upper part of the door to see if we were ready for coffee and sandwiches. Having been specific in saying ' Don't come into the room until the lights are on.' She saw an old man sitting on the arm of a chair, in which a woman sat. Then Margot counted and found it came to thirteen people, so she placed another plate, cup and saucer on the trolley. Later, when I questioned her about this, she told me about the old man. He was the father of the woman sitting in the chair, and he had been dead three years."

" What about ghosts ? Have you personally seen any ?"

" My father, Frederick Rowley Lake, was a director of James Hawker, the wine merchants in Plymouth. He was a disbeliever. So I said to him ' In view of your disbelief, I'll come and haunt you if I go first, I'll come and blow you a kiss! But if you go first, you must come and see me . . . and let me see and smell that old Harris Tweed jacket you should have thrown away years ago.' It was a year after his death, and I was then living at Crantock and I came across him sleeping in a deckchair. He was wearing his old Harris Tweed jacket, his glasses had fallen on his lap and his panama hat had slipped forward . . . just as he'd been when he'd been with me at Crantock two years before."

I visited Withiel on a Tuesday morning and stayed for lunch. Later that same day a young woman and her husband called on Betty Lukey for the first time.

Four days later I met the young couple, Anna and John Gunning, who were then living at Mennabroom, a solitary 13th century farmhouse on Bodmin Moor. They ranched cattle and sheep and bred half Arab ponies from a pure Arab stallion. In the summer they took in visitors, mainly young people wanting to see Cornwall from the saddle.

"From the top of the farm you can ride for twenty miles across the heather, and visit lonely tors like Brown Willy, the highest in Cornwall; Carburrow Tor, the scene of ancient sacrifices and Black Magic rites; or Dozmary Pool . . . and the only sounds are the wind in the heather and the curlew's cry," explained their brochure. "To the south of the farm are rarely-trodden paths through great oak woods in the lovely Glyn Valley; or the peaceful country lanes leading to old-world villages like St. Neot, Polmenna and Ley. We usually take a picnic lunch and ride all day."

I came to Mennabroom in mid-afternoon: a wild winter's day, when rain swept across the moors and mist blotted out almost everything. Water ran across the tracks: frothy, gurgling little streams; wind-screen wipers worked every minute of the drive.

How did the Gunnings find out about Betty Lukey? What prompted them to go to Withiel?

"I glanced down the columns of *The Cornish Guardian* . . . something I don't normally do . . . it was just fate . . . Though we're interested in the occult and spiritualism" explained John, as we sat around the dining room table.

A room of immense character with whitewashed granite walls and a massive open stone fireplace. An electric light was tastefully concealed in a lobster pot, a rocking chair, oil painting of a horse, and the sketch of a Scottish deerhound. "It was the second time I'd been to a clairvoyant; I'd been to quite a famous one in London. Mrs. Lukey, I thought, was equally as good . . . the only difference was Mrs. Lukey charged much less!"

" She was uncannily accurate."

That was the concise, considered reckoning of Anna. "Mrs. Lukey definitely has the power of fortune telling. She knew nothing about us, yet, after talking only about animals for something like ten minutes, she got out the cards and began telling us a great deal about ourselves, our pasts and our present situations."

Anna is a blonde. Long strands of hair, at times, hid her face, a face you'd remember in a crowd.

For the next half hour the Gunnings told me of Betty Lukey's revelations ; many of them deeply intimate. In Anna's case, Betty Lukey had analysed a close family relationship. In John's, she had seen an entangled human situation.

" What about predictions ? Too early to tell ?"

" Mrs. Lukey said we'd be getting some money within the next few weeks. It wouldn't be from a friend or an inheritance. It would be a surprise. And were we surprised when an auctioneer rang up two days ago to say we hadn't cashed a cheque for £120 !

"There was a warning too," Anna went on. " 'Be careful,' Mrs. Lukey said, ' Here's your son and I can see a pond. Keep your eyes open.' Well, there isn't a pond, but there's a stream. It's funny, I used to say to John, before we had any children : ' When we have a family, we'll have to be careful with this stream . . . it could be dangerous.' And now this warning . . . about a potential danger that's always there."

" Are you psychic ?" I asked Anna.

" I sense things. I don't see things, but I get a feeling . . . There are two roads that we can take to get to Liskeard. I remember John taking one particular road one day, and I instinctively knew he'd made the wrong decision. ' We should have gone the other way,' but I said nothing. A little further on we had an accident . . . that's the only accident we've had, and, in a way, I knew it was coming . . . we'd taken the wrong road to Liskeard. No, I don't see things. I just sense that something's going to happen or someone is going to appear . . . "

FALMOUTH 18

Doomed Sailor

Lucretia Kelly and I sat in a four-sided shelter on Falmouth sea-front. Stone steps rose to a wooden bench. Before us stretched Falmouth Bay : a calm, vast, unruffled sheet of water, reminding me that this is the softer, gentler side of Cornwall. It was across this same stretch of water that journalist Robert Manley sailed his *Tinkerbelle*, the last miles of a single-handed voyage from Falmouth, Masschusetts, to Falmouth, Cornwall. It was here too that the Tall Ships race had begun.

Falmouth, sprawling at the mouth of a large inlet of sea, has a long nautical history. Sir Walter Raleigh knew the value of this harbour. Falmouth, for many years, was an appointed port for mail boats or packets ; they continued to call until 1850. The end of the packets meant a decline in Falmouth's trade, but the authorities responded with vision by building and extending the docks. The docks remain - an important factor in the local economy. Falmouth, too assumed a certain importance in the last War as a repair depot and centre for British and American navies, a fact Hitler's bombers did not overlook. In and around the town British and American troops trained and waited for D-Day.

Lucretia Kelly is a smartly dressed woman with brown eyes. She had sent me a photograph of herself, taken more than a quarter of a century ago, but I had recognised her as soon as she opened the door of her home. That photograph of the Penryn Accordion Band and this stone shelter were two threads in a story which had roused my curiosity and had brought me fifty miles to meet her.

Her story concerned Falmouth in 1940, a year of German conquests in Europe, of Dunkirk, and threatened invasion. During the day, Lucretia Kelly - then she was Miss Johns - worked in the bookbinding department of J. H. Lake and Co. Ltd., and in the evening, exchanging working clothes for a black and red uniform, black skirt, red blouse, black velvet bolero and red sash, she played the accordion in local dance halls. Those were nights when dancers were moving to music like *Roll Out the Barrel*, *There Goes My Dream*, *Somewhere in France*, *Boom*, *Good-bye Sally* and *Little Sir Echo*. There were seven in the band : four boys and three girls, five with accordions, one at the drums, another at the piano. It was a year in which Cornish cinema audiences saw Dorothy Lamour in *Typhoon*, Dickie Lupino in *Just William*, Tommy Trinder in *Laugh It Off*, Jack Buchanan in *The Gang's All Here* and Shirley Temple in *The Little Princess*.

One spring evening Lucretia Johns met a special young sailor.

" It was in the dance hall, then named the Winter Gardens Ballroom, but it really was the Polytechnic Hall ; he came up stage to ask for a request tune. He was fair, rather nice looking ; he came from up North, he told me, and that he had one sister, a hairdresser. He was aboard H.M.S. *Hunter*, then in Falmouth Docks, and after that we had several dates. On March 7th, the ship's company held a farewell dance at the Princess Pavilion, and being a naval dance, everybody went to it, so that the other dances were empty ; anyhow, our band had to play in the Winter Gardens and Mr. Conyngham, who ran the dances, made us play to an empty hall, but around nine o'clock he had a change of heart, and closed down . . . you can guess where I made for !

"The next night - *Hunter's* last ashore - Alan and I went for a walk and ended up here in this shelter. At one point in our conversation I turned to him to say something, and it was all I could do to stop myself from screaming, because Alan had turned into a skeleton. I turned away, and then forced myself to look and speak to him, and when I looked he was quite normal once again. I didn't tell him of my vision, as I didn't want to scare him, but I must have looked queer, because he asked me if I was all right, although I'd done my best to hide it. Alan was just the same after the vision. It seemed to have no effect on him."

Next day H.M.S. *Hunter* sailed from Falmouth. Then, on Saturday, April 10th, on the B.B.C's one o'clock lunchtime news, came the announcement of *Hunter's* sinking in a Norwegian fjord. Lucretia Kelly still vividly remembers the horror. " My family and I were sitting at lunch, and I stood up from the table and shouted : 'Alan is dead !' I frightened my mother, and, at the time, she must have thought I had gone out of my mind.

" There were one-hundred and fifty-six men on board and forty-eight were picked up, three being killed by the action, the rest drowned. I felt sure the vision was a presentiment of Alan's death and that our good-bye was really and truly good-bye for ever. I didn't check any list of those who had died, but I saw a photograph taken in Sweden of the survivors, sent here to a mother and father of a local boy, and, of course, Alan was not in the group."

Now all these years later, Lucretia Kelly was sitting on the same seat in the same shelter on Falmouth sea-front.

"It's the first time I've been back here. I've sat in other shelters, but never this one. All because of what happened that night, I suppose. In a way, it's a strange sensation sitting here again after all those years."

In less than half-an-hour Lucretia Kelly was experiencing even a stranger sensation.

"Alan Clayton was his name, wasn't it?" Marshall Soult, the manager of Briggs' shoe shop, in Church Street, who had served on H.M.S. *Hunter*, looked thoughtful. "I've got a suspicion he survived. I didn't know him all that well, mark you, but I've got an idea I saw him alive after *Hunter's* sinking."

Lucretia Kelly sank into the nearest chair. Bewilderment creased her face. "Don't tell me he's alive after all these years."

Marshall Soult carefully studied a photograph, a snapshot of a group of survivors. "No, he's not among them." Lucretia Kelly studied the faces too. "Your mother showed me this soon after it had happened . . ." Marshall Soult interrupted her. "But these aren't all the survivors. There must have been another twenty who weren't in this. Alan Clayton might be one of them . . ."

Later, Lucretia Kelly and I continued our conversation over a cup of tea at her home, Grove Cottage, in Swanpool Street.

"I still think he's dead," was Lucretia Kelly's opinion.

"Just a feeling, you know . . ."

"There's only one way to find out. I'll write to Naval Records."

Back in Tintagel, I wrote to the office of the Commodore, H.M.S. Drake, at Devonport. A Naval man had advised this as the best avenue of information. Four days later, I had a letter telling me my request for information regarding Able Seaman Alan Clayton had been forwarded to the Principal Director of Accounts (Naval), Branch 3D Enquiries, Warminster Road, Bath.

The following week I was out of Cornwall. A brown "On Her Majesty's Service" envelope was among the mail awaiting my return.

"I have examined the ship's ledger of H.M.S. *Hunter*," the letter read, "which was sunk during 1940, but an Able Seaman Alan Clayton does not appear as a member of the crew."

My line of enquiry now switched back to the starting point of Falmouth.

Lucretia Kelly, for her part, stuck to her story. Moreover, she insisted she had written to Alan Clayton during *Hunter's* time at Plymouth, and had received replies. Marshall Soult, on consulting another ex-*Hunter* sailor, confirmed that a Clayton was aboard. Both, though, confessed they didn't know the man well, and could not be certain about his christian name.

Once more I contacted Bath. Again the same reply: Alan Clayton was not a member of the crew on H.M.S. *Hunter's* last voyage. But this time came the admission that a Clayton was aboard - no rank or christian names were given.

For a third time, I approached the Naval authorities, asking for the christian names of the Clayton concerned. But, by this stage, official patience had worn thin: "I regret to say that information relating to serving and ex-service naval personnel is considered as confidential and cannot be disclosed without consent of the person concerned," the Director replied. "As you are unaware of Mr. Clayton's correct details, I am unable to help further with your enquiry."

Was Alan Clayton aboard H.M.S. *Hunter* on that final, doomed expedition? Or was the Clayton mentioned by Records another man? Was Lucretia Kelly perhaps given an assumed name? And - either way - did Clayton survive?

I recall reading a poem some time ago, the last line of which was a row of question marks. Such an ending might be suitable for this chapter. But inevitably the last word must be Lucretia Kelly's: "I still insist I wrote and had replies. My one big regret now is that I did not keep his number . . . that would have been proof for anyone, but I never thought my story would be of interest in years to come."

NEAR CROWLAS 19

Premonition

I looked down the hill into the village of Crowlas and remembered Denys Val Baker's motoring experience.

One of Cornwall's best known authors and the editor of *The Cornish Review* he was, at the time, living at The Old Sawmills, Golant, up a creek off the River Fowey, but the incident had occurred, late one Saturday night, on this slanting piece of road which leads from Hayle to Penzance. He though had been travelling in the opposite direction - a nasty, nearly fatal accident it had been.

" We had been to a party at Newlyn," Denys Val Baker recalled, " I'd had an uneasy, uncomfortable feeling all day ; I hadn't really wanted to go to the party at all, but the others, Jess, my wife, Genevieve, my daughter, and a young friend, persuaded me, so we went. I was driving the Vauxhall Viva . . . everything perfectly normal . . . except that I was very subdued, had been so, in fact, all the evening . . . when suddenly the front right tyre went. The car turned broadside and rolled over twice. We ended up in West Cornwall Hospital ; and were lucky not to have been more seriously injured I suppose.

" And this isn't the first time, I've had this sense of premonition, almost an unconscious awareness of impending disaster. There was a case a few years ago, another party. My wife and I had been invited to one at a cottage on the cliffs at Cape Cornwall. About a week before the party, a friend of ours rang up, warning Jess not to go. ' I've had a premonition, for two nights running, I've had the same dream, I've seen you falling.' Eddy, being Cornish, we thought was perhaps more subject to premonitions than most of us. All the same we thought about not going to the party, but in the end Jess shrugged her shoulders, saying ' If we don't go, we shall always be wondering what might have been.'

" When Eddy heard our decision, he decided to take some action. He persuaded the owner of the cottage to erect barriers and fences around the cottage, and on the evening, when Jess and I arrived at Cape Cornwall, Eddy was there to greet us, and before going indoors, he insisted on leading Jess to various danger spots : ' If you come out for a breath of air - this way, not that, keep away from this pathway and so on.'

" Eventually we went in and discovered the cottage had been transformed. It was one of those solid Cornish granite cottages, knocked into one enormous room giving us plenty of space. Chinese lanterns sparkled and a five-piece band played in one corner. There was plenty of food and drink and the air of a really enjoyable occasion.

" Jess and I had a dance, and soon she was relaxed and laughing. For the next dance, she passed on to an exhuberant friend who whirled her round and round. The dance ended and as I half-turned I heard a scream. The next moment there was chaos. A huge iron bar, used for curtaining off a recess, had fallen to the ground . . . and Jess was lying underneath in a pool of blood. The bar had fallen across the centre of her head, opening up several ugly wounds. We decided the situation was so serious that we'd drive straight to the hospital, nearly ten miles away at Penzance. There, Jess had four stitches inserted and was whisked off to the women's ward.

" Since that accident, we've often wondered why did Eddy dream that dream ? And why did we still go to the party despite warning ? We had imagined a premonition of falling from cliffs and not falling under the weight of an iron bar. And what would have happened if we had not gone to Cape Cornwall that night ?"

In his book *Adventures before Fifty* * Denys Val Baker has described another hint of approaching disaster, this time on the Isles of Scilly. He and a company of family and friends had sailed there in *Sanu*. An elderly motor fishing vessel she is the heroine of his book : *To Sea with Sanu.* They were spending a pleasant evening ashore at The New Inn, on Trescoe. The saloon there holds a special fascination for sailors in that its walls are studded with photographs of shipwrecks, vessels that have died around the islands. " The result," wrote Denys Val Baker, " is a macabre sight, indeed. Barques, ketches, schooners, cargo boats, yachts, motor-boats - there they all were in various postures of discomfort ; if not broken into pieces, then hanging from sharp rocks, or grounded for ever on big banks.

* Published by John Baker

" Did someone jokingly make the remark, that evening, 'Let's hope we're never up there ?' I don't know. But I do remember, curiously, being haunted - indeed possessed is not too strong a word for it - by a strong feeling of unease. Looking back I can see quite clearly now that I did not really want to leave *Sanu* and go ashore, that I had no pleasure about taking my friends into The New Inn (whereas I had expected really to enjoy showing them around) - and that I was ill at ease the whole hour and a half we were ashore. In short, at least as any believer in the psychic would tell you, I was receiving intimations of impending trouble and I should have had the sense to respond to them.

" But, of course, we close ourselves up with our material certitudes, and so I tried to shrug away this feeling of unease . . ."

Later that evening, when the Val Baker party steered their way out of the harbour and into the channel, somebody asked " Where's the boat ?"

" I shall never, never forget the traumatic moment when I peered ahead through the twilight and saw at once that *Sanu* was not where she should be. What I *expected* to see was the bright anchor light somewhere in the middle of the channel, with the outline of Cromwell Castle well over to starboard. What I actually saw was the firm outline of Cromwell Castle seemingly in the centre, and the anchor light, brightly burning, well over to the right, against a dark, menacing background of cliffs and rocks.

" 'She's aground !' I cried out in anguish. 'She's on the rocks !'

" She was too, high and dry on the rocks, and heeling over at an alarming angle of about fifty degrees, her lower deck still awash with water from a tide which was almost at its lowest, leaving about four feet around the hull."

A Welshman, born in Yorkshire and educated in Sussex, Denys Val Baker has lived in Cornwall for more than twenty years. The knowledge that he has been accused of over-dramatising Cornwall and her impact leaves him unperturbed.

" It's impossible, I think, to live here and not be touched by the atmosphere of the place. It's a land of mystery, it's drenched in mythology. Writers and artists of all kinds have been influenced by this strange, brooding, almost compelling quality."

Clairvoyant Betty Lukey at Withiel: "One picks up something in the ether. We don't realise how much is in the atmosphere . . . it's a matter of tuning in to vibrations . . ." Chapter 17

Author Denys Val Baker of St. Buryan : " I'd had an uneasy, uncomfortable feeling all day . . ." Chapter 19

The road to Tregeseal near St. Just: "I heard this clatter of hooves and the rumble of a carriage or coach." Chapter 20

The Baker family at St. Buryan: "One's dealing with the unknown."
Chapter 21

His fund of memories contains something more serious, more tragic than his own string of premonitions. It concerned a friend called Len. " A young, witty, very-much-alive man," is how the author has painted him in words. " With Len around, the world became slightly enchanted. He was gay, charming, a delightful companion."

Friends though began to detect a change. Len started to wear a more haggard look. There was something washed out about him, and the Val Bakers, naturally concerned, persuaded him to explain why greyness had begun to envelope his personality.

Len, reminding them of the ancient Cornish superstition that when a bird taps at your window, your days are numbered, told how each morning, with the coming of dawn, a seagull regularly appeared at his window, how it tapped the window pane. " Have you ever seen a seagull's beak ?" asked Len. " It's long and curved and cruel, and looks like it's dipped in blood." No shooing worked on this particular gull. Habitually, as first light peeped over the horizon, he came to the window and began his tap . . . tap . . . tap.

" As Len told us the story, we were conscious of his curiously clouded eyes. We tried to pour cold water on the old superstition, but Len merely gave a tired smile : ' It's no use . . . it's just . . . fate !"

A few weeks later, Len was killed outright in a car crash. Denys Val Baker has a final memory of him.

" He had a companion with him, a young lad who was apparently far more badly injured. Yet Len looked almost untouched."

ST. JUST 20

Hoof-beats

"Tregeseal ¾ mile," said black letters on a white sign.

The car reached the bottom of the hill and I turned right. The road down the valley twisted out of sight. High and away to the left stood the outskirts of St. Just, its 15th century church tower dominant. Engine houses punctuated the bare, treeless landscape ahead. Beyond them stretched the vast blue face of the Atlantic; a ship nosed her way in the direction of the Bristol Channel. The wind howled and clouds hurried across the sky, yet March, that afternoon, was neither truly lion nor completely lamb. The sun was shining, the light crystal clear, and you understood why painters favour this region of Penwith, every feature standing out with a diamond sharpness.

I brought the car to a halt outside a farmhouse which backed on to the road. A dog bounded across the Macadam and peered into the window, his paws resting against the grey side of the car. Tex bared his teeth and snarled. Door of the car closed and Tex safely inside, I made my way round to the door on the other side of the house. Cattle were grazing in a sloping, sheltered field.

Phantom hoof beats had brought me these seventy-odd miles from Tintagel.

"I hear them coming down the road," explained Ethel Waters, a Cornish farmer's wife, who has lived at Chyoone Farm for twenty years. "They stop outside here, and it always happens in stormy weather. I heard them first soon after we came here to live. I heard this clatter of hooves and the rumble of a carriage or coach. A funny time to bring horses out, I thought. It was late at night, and the funny thing was I didn't hear them drive away. So, when it happened again, I checked up and went outside . . . nothing . . . no sign of horses or carriage or coach. But I definitely heard them come down the road. Certain of it. Funny thing is, I'm always alone when I hear them . . ."

"Could it be your imagination?" I interrupted.

Ethel Waters shook her head with conviction.

"I'm not the nervous type; my husband's a part-time fireman and I'm not worried about being left on my own. No, imagination doesn't come into it."

"How many times have you heard them?"

She looked thoughtful; her green eyes almost reflecting a sum of mental arithmetic.

"At least a dozen times, maybe twenty times. At first, I didn't take much notice of the noises; judging by the hoof beats, at least a couple of horses, I'd say. Some of my family, of course, are a bit cynical when I talk like this. And I've mentioned it to people outside the family. 'Oh, rubbish,' they say. But it isn't rubbish. We had an Alsatian dog, and when she heard the hooves she'd raise her heckles. That was proof enough for me . . . It wasn't dreaming or imagination. The dog heard them all right. These hoof beats don't alarm me in any way. I hear them coming down the road. I'd guess about two-hundred or three-hundred yards away, as if they're turning off the main road . . . and they always halt here."

"Why do they start here? Have you any theory?"

"Well, they say this was an old turnpike road, and perhaps there was a toll house here. After all, we're near the start of the road."

Turnpikes date, in fact, from the 17th century, when wheeled traffic was multiplying and there was anxiety about the condition of roads. Those, in authority, argued that the road-users should help to pay for the upkeep, and, on the strength of that argument, a number of Turnpike Acts were passed. First, local JPs, and later, boards of trustees, known as "Trusts," collected tolls by having barriers erected at certain points along the road. The original barriers were wooden bars, studded with pikes, which turned on a pivot - hence the term turnpike. But growth of the railways meant bankruptcy for the toll-gates, and by 1860 the great majority of them had vanished.

"And this road going down to Tregeseal could have been important," Ethel Waters continued. "Down at the end you'll find it meets five other roads, and one of them is the coast road to St. Ives. I'm only guessing about a toll-house being here, but I'm not guessing about *hearing* the horses. I've heard them too often for that . . ."

"Are you psychic?" I asked.

Ethel Waters looked thoughtful again.

"I think I'm a bit psychic. Some time ago I remember thinking about a Women's Institute medal my mother had won in London in 1920. I remembered thinking I'd like to have that one day. Then the next time I saw her she said: 'Ethel, you'd like to have that WI medal, would't you? Well, here it is.' She gave it to me, but I never asked for it.

"And then there have been several little things to do with television. I'm very fond of watching those quiz programmes, *Top of the Form* and *University Challenge*. I was watching the University programme one night with my elder son, and I said: 'Bamber Gascoigne is going to ask a question about music. He's going to ask who is the singer and what show does the song come from?' And the singer's going to be Topol, and the show's *Fiddler on the Roof*. And it just happened. I asked and answered the question just before he put it to the team. My son said it must be guesswork or that the programme was a repeat. But it was neither. Like the hoof beats, it can't be explained . . . it just happens. It's been several times, always television, never radio."

ST. BURYAN 21

Unexplained Noises

I met the Baker family in a semi-detached bungalow, approximately seven-hundred yards off the road which climbs from Lamorna to St. Buryan. Bernard James Baker is a bearded freelance electro-encephalographer (somebody who records and interprets the electrical activity of the human brain); his wife Celia is a former schoolteacher; and their son is called Scott. Their home, High Hopes, is built of Plymouth rock, an artificial stone of green and brown, it faces south-east and has a clear view of the Merry Maidens stone circle.

Though still in the Hundred of Penwith, my route on this return visit had taken me in a different direction. The weather too was different, a sullen day with the wind moaning and rain falling from a dark dome of sky.

A small advertisement in the personal column of *The Cornishman* was the genesis of my visit to High Hopes on a wild, wet March afternoon. " St. Buryan," the advertisement had read. " Mr. and Mrs. B. J. Baker reassure their local friends that they will not be driven out of their Moorcroft home by poltergeists or any other phenomena, though all accredited investigators will be warmly welcome." The cutting came to me via Peter Thomas, an old friend who farms at Truthwall on the other side of St. Just. " This might be worth investigating," he had suggested in his letter.

Indeed even outside a strictly supernatural context, this whole St. Buryan parish is worthy of investigation. Aged and weathered farms and cottages, tiny fields divided by granite hedges that almost give the impression of having grown out of the landscape; relics and reminders of both Bronze and Iron Ages are scattered over this windswept area. East of Boleigh you can find a fogou, one of those strange underground structures, lined and roofed with stone, which have mystified scholars and historians. Close to the tortuous B3315 you can see the Merry Maidens and the Pipers, stones that have been embroidered by imagination and legend. The Pipers, standing some fourteen feet, occupy a piece of high ground beyond a farm ; while the Maidens, a circle of stones, seventy-six feet across, are in a field, next to a derelict cottage, roughly half-a-mile from the musicians. Legend says they were dancing on a Sunday, and, for their sins, they were petrified into stone.

St. Buryan itself is basically a granite village. Its church tower dominates the countryside for miles, a simple, conspicuous landmark. The church is something of a surprise, unexpectedly large, for it was once a collegiate church with a dean and three prebendaries. Dedication is to either St. Berian or Beriana, an Irish maiden, the daughter of a Munster chieftain, who came to Cornwall sometime in the 5th century.

A modern building in this terrain is a faintly incongruous sight, and High Hopes, as it comes into view, is no exception. In such a setting you would have expected a crofter's cottage.

Bernard Baker and his wife sat opposite me, young Scott played with his toys on the floor. "The bungalow was built on land reclaimed from the moor. There's been no previous supernatural experience, the people in the house below have been living there since 1928 and they've experienced nothing like we've experienced in recent weeks. It all started on February 29th, 1968, when Celia was awoken by these unexplained noises around midnight.

" We've kept a fairly detailed record of the soundings, the conditions, etc." He handed me some notes and cuttings from two Westcountry newspapers. " No Poltergeist They Hope at High Hopes " was the headline of *The Cornishman*, and the opening sentence of an *Independent* reporter's story ran : " Thirty-nine-year-old Bernard Baker put a clock with a luminous dial beside his bed last week - so that he could make an accurate record of the happenings of ' the thing that goes bump in the night ' ".

My attention moved from the newspaper cuttings to the notes, written clearly in blue ink on unlined paper.

" The nocturnal noises began on February 29th, 1968.

" On the twenty-ninth of February and the first of March, 1968, Mr. Baker was woken up once each night (no wind, frosty and dull) at an uncertain hour, but thought to be after midnight - a loud initial ' thump ' (as though a length of stout timber had been driven gently by its end against the house wall outside), followed by similar softer ' thumps ' about every half to one minute, and with either light ' tapping ' or ' wood on stone ' scraping noises. Duration uncertain.

“ Night of the second and third of March, 1968. Mr. Baker was woken up at 11.30 p.m. by a loud ‘thump’ about every half to one minute (with the ‘scraping and tapping’ in between), and these noises continued until 12.15 a.m. Mr. Baker got out of bed and wandered silently about the house without any form of light whatever, and he noted that everywhere he went the noises were never at that particular place - noises seem to be immediately outside the house walls.

“ The noises having apparently ended at 12.15 a.m., Mr. Baker waited a few minutes and then opened the kitchen window and shone a powerful electric torch over the field in view, but nothing appeared to be out of place, garden gate was closed and there were no sounds of any kind, not even of distant cattle or vehicles.

“ Having retired, both Mr. and Mrs. Baker were this time awoken at about 1 a.m. by noises similar to the first two nights, also it appeared that Scott was also woken at the same time, since he started to cry as the parents awoke. The noises continued until 2 a.m. while Mr. and Mrs. Baker lay in bed feeling apprehensive. There was *no* wind and it was a rather dark night. At dawn, Mrs. Baker heard a shower of rain falling outside, which sounded perfectly natural.

“ Night of the eighth and ninth of March, 1968. Moonlight, frosty and no wind. At about 3.30 a.m. - 4 a.m., Mrs. Baker was woken by similar noises previously experienced, which lasted about five minutes, but then she fell off to sleep again. Later she was woken and this time Scott was also crying. Was Scott awoken by more noises? Mrs. Baker felt it was likely.

“ Night of the ninth and tenth of March, 1968. No sound of any wind, not particularly cold or especially moonlight - after midnight and possibly about 2.30 a.m. Mrs. Baker turned over in her sleep and clung to Mr. Baker's arm. This, in turn, woke him up (or was it a ‘bang or thump’?), and he was at once aware of the noises as before, which lasted two or three minutes.

“ Night of the thirteenth and fourteenth of March, 1968. Bright moonlight. (Full moon. Moderate,) gusty wind. Mr. Baker was awoken at 3.55 a.m., and was immediately aware of a ‘new’ sound, which occurred singly over the next three-quarters of an hour. This sound was of a ‘muffled low-pitched slap,’ rather as though a piece of flat timber (e.g. 2 ins x 18 ins x 18 ins.) was being dropped on its flat face upon a grass lawn. It occurred about ten to fifteen times at irregular intervals. No noises appeared to come from that side of the property which was brilliantly floodlit by the moon.

" Night of the twenty-first and twenty-second of March, 1968. Dark night, but only a light wind and possibly very slight rainfall. Starting at 9.45 p.m., there were heavy single noises (halfway between a ' thump ' and a ' crack '), which continued irregularly, and at 11.30 p.m. Scott was woken by them. The noises continued, and eventually, after midnight, Mr. Baker fell asleep for the first time. Between 1 - 2 a.m., Scott was woken up again and Mrs. Baker went to him, and on each occasion took some time to settle him down. The noises went on while Mrs. Baker was attending to Scott, and they continued for at least a half hour because Mr. Baker was still awake, though finally he fell asleep, despite the noises. Somewhere between 3 - 4 a.m., Mrs. Baker was woken by foot cramp and was immediately aware that the sounds were continuing. At 6.50 a.m., both Mr. Baker and Scott were awoken by what seemed to Mr. Baker a very loud single ' cracking thump,' but this was the last noise.'

I folded the notes back into their creases. " Do you believe in the supernatural ?" I asked Bernard Baker.

He sat in silence for several seconds.

" I'm open-minded on the subject, really."

" I'm the same," added his wife. " But in our own experience here at High Hopes there's no explanation. It's extraordinary, we've looked for an explanation, but we can't find one."

" Some people might interpret your advertisement in *The Cornishman* as an admission that this is somebody being a nuisance, somebody who wants you out of the bungalow, and nothing to do with the supernatural ?"

" There were two reasons for the advertisement," reflected Bernard Baker. " We are genuinely wanting help. If any psychic investigator can solve the problem, we shall be grateful ; if, on the other hand, it is somebody being a nuisance, it'll show him or her that we have no intention of leaving.

" We're strangers in a strange land ; this could conceivably happen in an isolated place like this ; we're more or less cut off. Somebody may be harbouring a grudge or be of a joking nature. If it is a joke, then it's hardly the behaviour of a balanced person, and such a person can be getting very little sleep."

" What about the people in the next-door bungalow ?"

" They're very heavy sleepers, apparently ; and, after the advertisement appeared in *The Cornishman*, we talked to them about it, but they said they'd heard nothing."

" Are you good sleepers ?"

" I die," Celia Baker admitted, with a smile.

" I fluctuate," said her husband.

My thoughts went back to the incidents concerning Cleave Camp and the cottage at Rame ; in both instances the death of a person had been involved.

" Have you had a death in the family ?" I enquired.

Celia Baker replied : " Yes, my father died on March 13th, after about a fortnight's illness . . . I suppose you could say his final illness coincided roughly with the beginning of these noises at High Hopes . . . though he'd been failing in old age - he was seventy-four - for about two years."

" What's the reaction of local people ?"

" Reaction varies enormously. Some people are quite open-minded and sympathetic, while others are completely disbelieving. We had an unexpected Robert Forbes, of the BBC, one evening, and the word must have got around. Anyway, when he was returning to his car around eleven o'clock, somebody leapt out at him, wearing a white sheet !"

" Do you think these sounds could possibly be caused by animals ?"

" No. Definitely not animal noises. The things we hear are like the sound of taps or a soft scraping, like wood on stone."

" Have you gone outside and investigated ?"

" No," Bernard Baker confessed. " I'm not the heroic type. Dressed in only pyjamas and dressing gown, you're fairly vulnerable, and if one had to tackle a mentally unbalanced person, I'd prefer to be more substantially dressed. Put it down to cowardice if you like. One's dealing with the unknown. It's either an unbalanced person or some supernatural force."

" We're not in a state of terror," said Mrs. Baker, " but one feels apprehensive. We've opened the kitchen window and the door, but we haven't ventured any further."

" Have you seen anybody, anything or any kind of form ?"

" No, but we've felt a slight physical vibration of the building."

Ten minutes later, I was walking through the wind and the rain to the car, mud, in places, sucking at my shoes. As I took a final backward look at the bungalow below, I felt genuinely sorry for the family, whose home it is. " What would you do in their shoes ?" I asked myself. " Ask for a service of exorcism, in the hope of removing some evil spirit ? Or seek the services of a psychic investigator, preferably a Spiritualist ? Or merely call in the Police ?"

POSTSCRIPT

"There's always the problem of knowing how and when to finish." Wallace Nichols, the author, was sitting in a chair that once belonged to Shelley, talking about poetry. "There should," he said, "be a moment, to the technician, when he *knows* it is obligatory to abstain."

This journey across Cornwall in search of the supernatural has been far removed from putting a poem into shape, but ten years later or thereabouts, with Wallace's bones now lying in Madron cemetery, I begin to understand the significance of his words. Certainly bringing some of these interviews to a close has been difficult, more difficult than politely halting a conversation, for a handshake and a good-bye at the door has not always been the end of the story.

Information has kept filtering through. David Waddon-Martyn, for example, has had further experiences since our conversation at Tonacombe; sadly one of Alan Nance's patients has passed away (the others are fit and well, no longer patients in the real sense of the word). Then clairvoyant Betty Lukey, on my suggestion, met Northcountry actor Geoffrey Tomlin who was holidaying in Cornwall; she gave him a date to 'star' in his diary. Months later he rang to say that his television career, on the very day, had received a substantial and completely unplanned boost! Perhaps most incredible of all, Lucretia Kelly, her curiosity stirred, did some amateur detective work and discovered that Alan Clayton did not drown in that Norwegian fjord back in 1940. Moreover since our meeting on Falmouth seafront, the couple and their families have met, proving - if we needed reminding - that fact can appear more ficticious that fiction itself.

These are only some of the events in the chain.

It may seem a cliche, but today is truly the daughter of yesterday: Life goes on, one experience leading to another. Indeed on the strength of this journey, I am more convinced than ever that the thing we call death is not the end but merely another door opening.

I cannot honestly write a final full-stop because I believe no such thing exists.

Acknowledgements

Many people have made this book possible - some by writing letters and providing information, others by granting interviews and allowing me to visit their properties. They are too numerous to list here, but I sincerely thank them for their co-operation.

My thanks also to James Turner for his encouragement and help; to the various Westcountry newspapers who initially publicised my search for supernatural experience; to Angela du Maurier and her publisher Peter Davies for permission to quote from her book *Old Maids Remember*; Denys Val Baker and John Baker to quote from *To Sea with Sanu*; and to the four photographers for providing the illustrations - with one exception every photograph was taken especially for this publication.

Finally, I am once more deeply grateful to Barbara Escott for her painstaking editorial work on the manuscript and reading of the proofs.

ALSO AVAILABLE

CHARLES, DUKE OF CORNWALL

by Michael Williams. 30 photographs. Price 75p.

'This, the first ever publication about Prince Charles in his role as Duke of Cornwall is full of character and interest. There are recollections of people who have met him, accounts of visits to the Westcountry, his service training in the south-west, at Dartmouth and Yeovilton; fascinating facts and figures about the Duchy of Cornwall which stretches across six counties and has made the Prince one of the wealthiest young men in the world. A story that will appeal to all Westcountry people – and Royalists everywhere.'

David Clarke, Cornish Life

MY DARTMOOR

by Clive Gunnell of Westward TV – television's most famous walker. Price 95p. Map and 12 pages of photographs and drawings of Dartmoor wildlife by Robin Armstrong. Introduction by Jeremy Thorpe, M.P.

'... a winner all the way.' Express & Echo

'The work is that of a merry man, and an observant, though kindly one.'
Western Morning News

'An excellent book.' Kenneth MacLeod on Westward TV

'... fascinating reading ...' Plymouth Times

'Clive Gunnell and the Moor ... the love affair that will never end ...'
Jim Dalrymple, The Independent

TIGHTLINES SOUTH WEST

A fishing guide to the south west by the popular Westcountry and Westward TV angler. Drawings and photographs – a mine of information for the angler, both local and visitors. Price 95p.

'A book with Tightlines South West as its title can only have been written by one person. And Ted Tuckerman doesn't disappoint us. He shares his vast knowledge of angling and where to fish our local shores and wrecks.'

Jack White, Sunday Independent

MY CORNWALL

A personal vision of Cornwall by eleven writers living and working in the county: Daphne du Maurier, Ronald Duncan, James Turner, Angela du Maurier, Jack Clemo, Denys Val Baker, Colin Wilson, C. C. Vyvyan, Arthur Caddick, Michael Williams and Derek Tangye with reproductions of paintings by Margo Maeckelberghe and photographs by Bryan Russell. Price 95p.

'An ambitious collection of chapters.' The Times, London

ALONG THE LEMON

by Judy Chard. 35 photographs and map. Price 75p.

The lifestory of a Dartmoor river by the well-known Devon novelist and short story writer who lives alongside it. Judy Chard puts one of Devon's lesser-known rivers on the map, tracing its journey from below Haytor to where it meets the Teign at Newton Abbot.

DEVON MYSTERIES

by Judy Chard. Price £1.

An exploration of strange happenings, ranging from hauntings and the man they couldn't hang to UFOs.

OCCULT IN THE WEST

by Michael Williams.

Investigations and interviews relating to the Occult in Devon and Cornwall. Ghosts and clairvoyancy, dreams and psychic paintings, hypnosis and healing are only some of the facets of a fascinating story.

KING ARTHUR COUNTRY in CORNWALL, THE SEARCH for the REAL ARTHUR

by Brenda Duxbury, Michael Williams and Colin Wilson.
Price £2.95 hardcovers. £1.20 softcovers.

An exciting exploration of the Arthurian sites in Cornwall and Scilly.

'The best Bossiney book so far ...' Cornish Life

CORNWALL & SCILLY PECULIAR

by David Mudd. Price £1.00

Some of the people, events, values and beliefs that create the background to Cornwall's strange and compelling charm.

'*... one of the most important titles produced by Bossiney ...*' The Cornishman

ABOUT WIDECOMBE

by Judy Chard. 43 photographs. Price 90p.

'A warmly recommended read for all who love Devon - and Dartmoor in particular.'
The Independent

DOWN ALONG CAMBORNE AND REDRUTH

by David Mudd. 44 illustrations. Price 95p.

'spicy but informative ... extremely good value.'

Robert Jobson, Camborne-Redruth Packet

'his journalist's eyes and ears and his sympathy ... add to the reader's understanding ...' West Briton

THE FALMOUTH PACKETS

by David Mudd. 25 illustrations. Price 65p.

'... the only history of the Falmouth Packet ships to be written in this century ... vivid and lively...' Enid Thompson, Western Morning News

'An exciting story, lovingly told ...' The Falmouth Packet

POLDARK COUNTRY

by David Clarke – published in conjunction with Cornish Life magazine. Over 40 photographs of Cornwall's Poldark Country. Fascinating facts about the Cornish past. Locations used for the TV series and interviews with Winston Graham and the cast. Price 75p.

THE BARBICAN

by Elizabeth Gunnell. 32 photographs. Price 65p.

These words and pictures will help you to enjoy the Barbican that bit more – and reveal something of the spirit of the people and the place.

ALONG THE CAMEL

by Brenda Duxbury and Michael Williams. Price 65p.

'... it is well written, attractively presented, full of historical facts ...'
'Worth a place on anyone's bookshelf.' Western Evening Herald

ABOUT ST IVES

A portrait in words and pictures of the ancient Borough. By Elizabeth Sparrow & Michael Williams. Peopled with fascinating characters and events, ancient and modern. Price 50p.

'... a fascinating and tremendously readable work concentrating on the history and the artists of the little town ... and have devoted a section to some of the interesting walks to be taken in the area.' The Cornishman

THE LIZARD

by Jill Newton of St Keverne. Price 75p.

An exploration of the famous Cornish peninsula in words and pictures.

TOTNES

Elizabeth Gunnell follows the success of her Barbican story with an immensely readable guide about Totnes, one of the oldest boroughs in Britain. Price 65p.

ABOUT LOOE

Austin Toms, a member of the well-known Looe family, talks to Brenda Duxbury about old Looe – while Brenda herself explores Looe and district today. Price 65p.

PENZANCE TO LAND'S END

by Michael Williams and John Chard.

A journey in words and pictures – brilliant photography by John Chard – incorporating Newlyn, Mousehole, Lamorna and Porthcurno.

ABOUT MEVAGISSEY

by Brenda Duxbury.

Where to go and what to see in and about Mevagissey today.

MAKING POLDARK

by Robin Ellis. Over 60 photographs. Price 75p.

The inside story of the popular BBC TV series.

'... an interesting insight into the making of the TV series ...'

Camborne Redruth Packet

'It is a "proper job", as they say, and a credit to all concerned.'

Archer in Cornwall Courier

CORNISH SEA LIGHTS

by David Mudd. 29 illustrations and map. Price 75p.

In this his Bossiney hat-trick, David Mudd pilots his readers afloat and aloft with the story of notable Cornish lighthouses, lightships, designers and builders in a factual account of courage, enterprise, danger and intrigue.

'... will be enjoyed by all those who relish tales of triumph over adversity ...'

The West Briton

TO TAVISTOCK GOOSIE FAIR

by Clive Gunnell. Over 30 illustrations. Price 65p.

Clive Gunnell brings to life one of the country's most historic fairs, introduces us to some of the characters who make it such an event and takes us on a personal conducted tour of the ancient Stannary Town.

If you have any difficulty in obtaining our titles, write direct to Bossiney Books, Land's End, St Teath, Bodmin, Cornwall – adding 15p for p + p for each copy.

We shall be pleased to let you have a full list of our titles and details of forthcoming publications.